Closing the Achievement Gap

NO EXCUSES

Patricia Davenport
Gerald Anderson, Ed.D.

AMERICAN PRODUCTIVITY
& QUALITY CENTER

EDUCATION INITIATIVE

American Productivity & Quality Center
123 North Post Oak Lane, Third Floor
Houston, Texas 77024

Edited by Craig Henderson and Barbara Peyton
Designed by Connie Choate

Manufactured in the United States of America

ISBN 1-928593-62-3

American Productivity & Quality Center
Web site address: www.apqc.org

Dedication

The authors dedicate this book to the people of Brazosport Independent School District in southeastern Texas:

- *the parents who had the courage to question the education their children were receiving;*
- *the school board members who responded by saying, "That's not right; fix it!";*
- *the administrators who accepted the challenges and provided the leadership to change the system;*
- *the teachers who embraced the theory that all children can learn and who refused to lower the standard for any child; and*
- *the students who gave us the ultimate proof—reflected in test data.*

Contents

Foreword

The famous professional baseball player, Dizzy Dean, was once accused of bragging about his pitching accomplishments. He responded to the accusation by saying, "If you did it, it ain't bragging." The story of the marvelous increases in student achievement that occurred in the Brazosport Independent School District in Texas during the 1990s might be seen by some as a form of bragging by the authors. Those critics need to be reminded of the immortal words of Dizzy Dean, for the authors were the leaders who "did it."

I am honored to write the foreword to this book because the Brazosport story provides two critical ingredients that school reformers need now more than ever: hope and a map to follow.

We know that the number of poor and disadvantaged students continues to increase as a percentage of the total K–12 population. In most places, these students aren't achieving in school. We have been told that these students can't or won't learn. We feel defeated and trapped when we are held accountable for their learning. We need someone or something that gives us hope. Clearly, the increases in measured student achievement across all Brazosport schools and students, but especially among disadvantaged students, should serve as a source of hope and inspiration for all who care about our children, their education, and the economic future of our country.

The hope that is reflected in the Brazosport story offers us a vision of what is possible. As important as that vision is, most of us still need a map that guides us to the realization of that vision. This book describes, in simple and straightforward steps, the processes that were used to propel the district forward on its journey toward continuous improvement. The vital role of critical elements—such as collaboration and empowerment, data-driven decision making, core beliefs and values, and leadership—are woven throughout the book.

I especially appreciate this presentation of the Brazosport story because it affirms and validates the Effective Schools research findings as well as school improvement processes based on it. We have known for a long time that Effective Schools research, when integrated with continuous improvement theory, represents a powerful approach for improving schools one at a time. From the large-scale reforms associated with this school district, we now know that the same framework can guide district-level reforms as well.

The challenge to you, the reader, is to find the hope and inspiration in the Brazosport story, study the map that the authors provide, and lead similar reform in your school or district. Who knows, maybe when your story is added to the large and growing body of successful school reform case studies, the belief that all children can learn will truly become the core belief for American public education.

— Lawrence W. Lezotte, Ph.D.
Educational Consultant

Preface

Our story begins on a hot summer evening in 1991 in a small community located on the Texas Gulf Coast, about 60 miles south of Houston. More than 200 parents had crowded into a tiny school board meeting room where I, as the newly appointed school superintendent, was to hold my first meeting.

How nice, I thought, that all of these people had come to welcome me. I soon learned, however, that this audience had a different agenda.

One of the parents, apparently designated to speak for the group, stood up. He raised a question that I was totally unprepared to answer and that would forever burn in my mind. "Dr. Anderson," he asked, "why is it that the students in the south-side schools aren't doing as well as the students on the north side?"

I knew instantly of what he was talking about. The newspaper had just published the test scores for the entire Brazosport Independent School District. Scores were low at schools in Clute and Freeport—where the poorer and minority students attended classes. Scores were decidedly higher in the more prosperous Lake Jackson area, on the north side of the district.

"Dr. Anderson, perhaps you didn't hear me. Why are the students in the south side not doing as well as the students on the north side?"

What could I say? That the students in Freeport are not as smart as those in Lake Jackson? That the teachers in Freeport are not as good as those in Lake Jackson?

No way.

For the moment, I was saved by Texas school board procedure, which does not require a response to questions raised in an open meeting. I replied simply, "Next item on the agenda."

After the meeting, one of the school board members, who worked at Dow Chemical, set me straight. "Jerry, if we ran our business the way this district is run, we'd be out of business in a year."

He invited me to his office to tell me about Total Quality, a proven business method based on continuous improvement. The journey described in this book began that night. It ended nine years later like this:

- students in the Freeport schools performing just as well, if not better, than students in the Lake Jackson schools regardless of race, gender, or socioeconomic condition;
- the district's dropout rate declining from about 6 percent to one-tenth of 1 percent;
- Brazosport receiving the 1998 Texas Quality Award, a prestigious honor normally reserved for businesses;
- Brazosport becoming a finalist in the education category of the 1999 Malcolm Baldrige National Quality Award; and
- my being named Superintendent of the Year by the Texas Association of School Boards/Texas Association of School Administrators.

The journey from that school board meeting to those achievements was not made overnight. It was long and difficult. And it required the cooperation and leadership of administrators, parents, teachers, and school board members. The journey is not over yet.

Patricia Davenport, who served as director of curriculum and instruction during my tenure at Brazosport, was instrumental in our successful turnaround. She now joins me as collaborator on this book. We have both moved on from our administrative posts at Brazosport to devote our energies full time to telling this story at conferences, on site visits, and in publications. We tell it because we know that other schools can benefit from what we have learned. And, as we share our experiences, we also learn and take with us new ideas. Our message is simple: There are no excuses for low student performance. All students can learn. All teachers can teach.

This book describes the steps that we followed to achieve amazing results. No magic formula. No design model. No miracles. *No excuses.*

Here's what we did.

Part I:

The Brazosport Journey
to Equity and Excellence

Chapter 1

Accountability Started It All

Accountability got us started 10 years ago, but it isn't account-ability that drives us today. The 1,300 employees of Brazosport Independent School District now have a deeper conviction. They believe they can teach every child and help each one reach higher and higher levels of academic achievement. The teachers believe this because they have seen it with their own eyes and because they understand their mission.

In fact, you can go up to any person on any campus in the school district today—whether it is a custodian, bus driver, teacher, aide, or principal—and ask him or her what the Brazosport School District is all about. With no hesitation, each will be able to tell you in simple, compelling, and measurable terms.

This book is about an experience that changed an entire district. It is a journey the men and women of the district traveled. It is story of how these men and women worked together to close a wide gap in student achievement levels. And it is the story of how Brazosport ISD became one of the highest-performing school districts in the state of Texas in only a few years.

While exam scores and school labels might have motivated us originally, today we understand that our mission is one of a far greater calling: to be exemplary in every way and to help each child reach his or her potential.

While all 50 states now require students to submit to a state assessment, Texas was one of the first states in the nation to implement a rigorous accountability system using achievement standards, tests to measure whether or not students had met the standards, and a rating system based on test scores and other factors.

In 1990 Texas lawmakers sent a powerful message to educators. They demanded that the state's schools teach *all* children and insisted that no child or group be left behind. The legislation evolved from earlier efforts of some of the state's most influential CEOs, including Ross Perot, who were convinced that Texas schools could apply successful business practices to education to improve student performance. Ultimately, they wanted to help students prepare to meet the demands of a changing and technology-driven work force.

Naturally, many of us working as educators did not appreciate business leaders and lawmakers meddling in our domain. Armed with our own stacks of research, we argued that the rules of business did not necessarily apply to education and that the state could be headed for some serious trouble. Nevertheless, the Texas legislature in 1995 moved forward with a sweeping school reform package that was implemented by the Texas Education Agency, or TEA as it's known.

Emerging from this reform was a school ratings system based chiefly on scores from the Texas Assessment of Academic Skills (TAAS), a series of tests in reading, writing, and math administered annually to students in grades three through eight and grade 10. While schools were allowed to exempt students with limited English proficiency or with special-education needs, no allowances were made for a school's socioeconomic or demographic makeup. A formula based on TAAS scores, dropout rates, and attendance records then determined whether a school's own "report card" would be classified as "exemplary," "recognized," "acceptable," or "low-performing." A school can be classified as exemplary only if 90 percent or more of students of all ethnic groups and socioeconomic strata are successful in passing each subject area of the TAAS. No student groups are exempt. Additionally, a school cannot achieve exemplary status unless its dropout rate for all student groups is less than 1 percent.

A variety of rewards and sanctions were put in place to recognize individual school performance. These ranged from cash awards for exemplary schools to public hearings and eventual closings for low-performing schools. In addition to reporting their new classifications, schools were required to publish their cumulative test scores as well as those of their subgroups, such as economically disadvantaged or minority students, in local papers.

There was another critical feature of the school reform package. While individual schools would be held accountable for student performance, the school district as a whole was granted new autonomy and the freedom to find innovative ways to raise student achievement.

Chapter 2

Day of Reckoning

It was against this backdrop and just as the first TAAS report had been published in the local newspaper that an unusually large group of parents filed into the board room of the Brazosport Independent School District in the summer of 1991.

About 250 in all, they represented the diverse economic background of this coastal community 60 miles south of Houston—fishermen and shrimpers who cast their nets into Texas' deep-water Gulf; employees from two nearby prisons; physicians, nurses, and staff members of the area's clinics and hospitals; and a host of teachers and professors from area schools and the local community college. Also present were a large number of operators, engineers, and managers from the county's four major chemical plants: Dow Chemical, BASF, Shintech, and Rhodia.

They came from eight neighboring cities: Clute, Freeport, Jones Creek, Lake Jackson, Oyster Creek, Quintana, Richwood, and Surfside—all located near the Brazos River. Varying in size from less than 100 people to more than 25,000, these communities had joined together some 50 years earlier to form a single school district that would serve about 13,000 students on 18 campuses. These parents also represented the district's rich ethnic diversity; 55 percent of the students were white, 34 percent Hispanic, and 9 percent African American.

The meeting on this hot and humid summer evening just happened to coincide with the arrival of the district's new superintendent, Gerald Anderson, who was under the optimistic, but clearly mistaken impression that the gathering would amount to an incredible community welcome.

He quickly realized that the parents had not come to socialize. They were angry and wanted to voice their frustration over the district's recently published ratings. Earlier in the week *The Facts* had reported that nine of the district's 18 schools had been classified as "low-performing," the lowest possible rating and below the minimum requirements for even an "acceptable" rating. (The TAAS "acceptable" level at the time required a passing rate of 25 percent to 69 percent on test scores, a 3.5 percent to 5.9 percent dropout rate, and a 94 percent attendance rate.) For the first time in the district's history, an abundance of data clearly indicated that those schools with large percentages of economically disadvantaged students scored far lower than those schools having only a few poor students.

While about 40 percent of all students were classified as economically disadvantaged, the students were dispersed throughout the schools in a disproportionate way. For example, fewer than 10 percent of the students in Beutel Elementary were classified as economically disadvantaged, while more than 80 percent were so designated at Velasco Elementary.

Questions flew one after the other:

"Why are African American students at Velasco Elementary passing the TAAS math test at a rate of 8.3 percent when white students are passing at 64.7 percent?"

"Why are the schools on the south side not doing as well as the schools in the north?"

"Dr. Anderson, perhaps you didn't hear me. Why are the students on the south side not doing as well as the students on the north side?"

Fortunately, in Texas one does not have to answer questions during the open forum portion of a board meeting. So Gerald moved on to the next agenda item while silently pledging to look into the situation and come back with answers.

Several of the school board members stayed after the meeting to give Gerald the bottom line: The district was doing a dismal job of teaching its poor children, and something had to be done to turn things around.

One of the members, Joe Bowman from Dow Chemical, the largest employer in the area, was even more frank. "Jerry, if we made the excuses in our business like you guys make in your business, we'd be flat broke and out of business in a year. You need to stop making excuses and find a way to teach these children."

He then provided a ray of hope. He suggested that the district might learn from what Dow had done years earlier when it implemented a comprehensive quality control program throughout its 5,000-acre complex. The improvements at Dow were so transforming that they had even caught the company's management by surprise.

Other board members agreed that the district might get big-time results using Dow's approach to quality. Jesse Hibbetts, a Dow employee and board member at the time, arranged for Gerald Anderson to attend W. Edwards Deming's training. The board members offered to underwrite Total Quality Management (TQM) training for the new superintendent and his chief reports.

Looking back on that evening, without the accountability pressure and the requirement that all subgroups have the same proportionality, Brazosport might never have found the resolve and the ability to begin the arduous process of change. Accountability shocked the district into action.

And while accountability was the impetus for our first few years, it is now much more intrinsic. The focus is not on what has been accomplished but instead on continuous improvement.

Chapter 3

Going Slow at First

We started slowly, but that's one of the principles of TQM: Go slow at first, so you can go fast later.

And, of course, we had our preconceived notions about how Dow Chemical or any company for that matter could be of help. What did Dow's quality program, which the company called the Managing Breakthrough Process, have to do with us?

Educators have reservations about applying business teachings and best practices to schools for a variety of reasons. Among them, we are suspicious of business motives. We sometimes think business doesn't understand education at all. We don't know how to apply business tools to education. And we certainly don't think business should try to tell us what to do.

We're not even in agreement about who our customers are. We once spent two weeks settling a debate that went something like this: One group argued that our primary customers were the parents. After all, they send us their best and we have to make them happy. Another group argued that our primary customers were the employers in our community who pay the bulk of the ad valorem taxes to our schools. Finally, an elementary teacher stood up and said, "I am tired of this. The primary customer is the student."

There was silence. We thought, "Who does this second grade teacher think she is?" But she was right. The primary customer is the student, and everyone else is an external customer. You certainly have to please your taxpayers and your parents. But, in regard to student outcomes, we were sharing the data with everybody but the primary customer. We had discussed the data with the school board. We had discussed it with the parents. We even discussed it with the teachers. But we had never sat down with a child one-on-one to say,

"According to your test results, these are your strengths, and these are the areas you need to work on."

So, with a certain amount of trepidation, we accepted the challenge to begin quality training. The plan was for Gerald to take the course first and then for the district's management team—which consisted of principals, central office directors, and lead teachers—to follow. While we were apprehensive, we also recognized that business is often the driver for change. And we had all been convinced during the school board meeting and the days that followed that change was just what Brazosport ISD needed.

We were about to understand how TQM could enable the district to become more data-driven, process-oriented, and effective—that we must solve problems, not ignore them. We would understand, in business terms, that our primary stakeholder was the student and our product was student achievement.

The first thing we learned was to resist attaching blame. In quality, you don't fix blame; you fix the system. As we began the training, we were all in agreement about one thing: We had already spent way too much time and too much energy blaming others for our problems. We were determined to stop doing that.

Our mission was to envision how quality principles, along with the Effective Schools philosophy to which Gerald already adhered, could be integrated in a management system that addressed both equity and excellence.

Chapter 4

No Excuses, Just Effective Schools

In the fall of 1991 Brazosport Independent School District unfortunately held not only the distinction as a low-performing school district but also as a high-cost one. After the TAAS scores were published in *The Facts,* many in the community wanted to know why they weren't getting a far better return on the investment of the county's large petrochemical tax base.

Most of these people were unaware of recent changes in the Texas school finance system, aptly named the "Robin Hood Plan," which gave the state authority to redistribute a percentage of taxes from its wealthier districts to its poorer ones.

Gerald thought he would explain to the local business community how the Robin Hood plan was literally "robbing" the district of its potential. It was responsible—well, at least partly responsible—for shortcomings in student performance. After all, without sufficient funding for much-needed tutors, technology, and other resources, how could test scores improve? But, as his presentation to community leaders neared, it occurred to Gerald that he was as guilty as anyone in making excuses for why some children did not seem to be learning in the current school system.

When he was a high school math teacher, Gerald had blamed a student's poor performance on the junior high math teacher. She, in turn, blamed the child's elementary teacher. The elementary school teacher blamed the parents, who obviously had not helped their child with homework. The parents, in turn, blamed it on the genes. The blame game was endless.

We often illustrate this cycle of blame in our seminars with the following poem by an anomymous author, titled "Who's to Blame":

The college professor said: "Such rawness in a student is a shame; lack of preparation in high school is to blame."

Said the high school teacher: "Good heavens! That boy's a fool. The fault, of course, is with the middle school."

The middle school teacher said: "From stupidity may I be spared. They sent him in so unprepared."

The primary teacher huffed: "Kindergarten blockheads all. They call that preparation? Why, it's worse than none at all."

The kindergarten teacher said: "Such lack of training never did I see. What kind of woman must that mother be."

The mother said: "Poor helpless child. He's not to blame. His father's people were all the same."

Said the father at the end of the line: "I doubt the rascal's even mine."

By now Gerald was developing a keener understanding of the district's problems. Deep down, he knew they didn't have a thing to do with Robin Hood, mediocre teachers, absent parents, or any other rationale. The answers were clearly evident in the TAAS reports.

One could easily trace the good scores to the "good schools" located on the north side of the district. Seventeen of the district's 18 campuses were in Lake Jackson, Clute, and Freeport. Schools in Lake Jackson served students from mostly a middle- to upper-middle-class economy, and only 10 percent of the student body was classified as economically disadvantaged. On the south side of the district, students from Clute and Freeport schools came from mostly low-income households. About 60 percent of the students in Clute schools, and as many as 85 percent of the students in Freeport schools were classified as economically disadvantaged (Figure 1).

The TAAS scores and subsequent ratings clearly indicated that those schools containing a large percentage of economically disadvantaged students were not performing as well as schools in more affluent areas. Equally as important, the data revealed that the results were not linked to race or ethnicity. They were simply tied to the economics of the household.

TAAS Passing Rates
Freeport Intermediate

Reading	92–93	93–94	94–95	95–96	96–97	97–98	98–99	99–00	00–01
All Students	62.7%	72.6%	69.9%	82.7%	90.8%	94.9%	94.4%	93.4%	98.1%
African American	53.8%	65.6%	59.1%	80.8%	80.3%	94.3%	88.2%	96.7%	95.6%
Hispanic	52.1%	64.6%	63.3%	75.6%	90.3%	93.5%	92.9%	88.8%	97.7%
White	80.2%	82.1%	82.6%	92.4%	94.9%	96.7%	98.4%	98.9%	99.4%
Economically Disadvantaged	47.6%	64.0%	61.6%	75.8%	88.1%	92.1%	92.3%	90.9%	97.4%

DEMOGRAPHICS:

Economically Disadvantaged	62.9%	African American	10.4%
Limited English Proficiency	4.2%	Hispanic	51.3%
Mobility	20.2%	White	37.8%

Figure 1

Gerald was not about to tell the leadership of this community that poor children could not be taught. He knew better. In the summer of 1966, just after his own college graduation, he remembered the impact that the Coleman Report had made on education.

Dr. James Coleman, then a professor at Johns Hopkins University, and Ernest Campbell of Vanderbilt University presented a report to the U.S. Congress asserting that academic achievement was strongly related to family background in the early years and that "schools bring little to bear on a child's achievement independent of his background and general social context." Dr. Coleman further contended that attendance at segregated schools created an even greater disparity in academic achievement between the races. (The government used the report to support school busing, and it became a manual for political and court actions. In 1975 Dr. Coleman withdrew his support of busing after finding in another study that it encouraged "white flight.")

A team of researchers from Michigan State University took issue with Coleman's conclusions. Convinced there was something wrong with the report, Professors Larry Lezotte, Ron Edmonds, and Wilber

Brookover launched an investigation of their own. Simply put, they wanted to know why some schools are effective and others are not.

Their efforts would turn Professor Coleman's conclusions upside down. The researchers found two types of schools that Coleman's research would have contended could not exist. The first were highly effective schools that served mainly students from low- and middle-income families. Second were schools with dismal performance records that served children from middle- and upper-income families.

The researchers identified five characteristics—or correlates—common to all effective schools:

1. Strong instructional leadership by the principal that frames the school's vision and turns it into reality
2. High expectations of student achievement by students and staff members
3. A broadly understood instructional focus that centers on reading, writing, and mathematics
4. A safe and orderly school climate conducive to teaching and learning
5. Frequent measures of pupil achievement as a basis for program evaluation and improvement

The Effective Schools Movement, as it would come to be known, presented impressive evidence that background was not a factor in a child's ability to succeed. Truly effective schools could teach all children. This did not mean that all children can learn at the same rate, on the same day, or in the same way. Instruction must be customized to meet each child's unique needs and abilities.

A new definition emerged from the movement. Effective schools have "equal proportions of low, middle, and high socioeconomic students attaining similarly high levels of mastery of the essential curriculum."

Effective Schools research sent an important wake-up call to educators: "No child should be condemned to educational failure because of his or her family background, race, or socioeconomic status."

The time to meet with the business community had arrived. Instead of using the Robin Hood plan to explain away the district's problems, Gerald began to talk about the Effective Schools research and what it could mean to Brazosport. It was a speech that would be repeated often from the board room, and to community groups, to PTA meetings, to classrooms throughout the area.

"You and I know that the business of teaching children is not a simple process," he would begin. "But, there is good reason to believe that we can start putting time and energy into a program that enables all children, regardless of race, ethnicity, family background, or socioeconomic status, to succeed."

The key, Gerald would explain, was to overcome old beliefs and barriers that leave poor children with a poor education. He would point to compelling research from Michigan that claimed that each and every school could succeed, regardless of its constituency.

"We have to reach down deep inside and question our own belief systems and values. Ultimately, we need to quit talking about why we can't do it and start talking about how we can. If we work together, we can get there."

Not surprisingly, the message was not greeted with enthusiasm in the beginning. Typical responses: "Doc, do you know the kind of kids we have?" or "We can't expect these poor kids in Freeport and Clute to do what the kids in Lake Jackson are doing."

Gerald would often quote the late Ron Edmonds, one of the principals of the Effective School movement, to answer these concerns:

"How many effective schools would you have to see to be persuaded of the educability of poor children? If your answer is more than one, then I submit that you have reasons of your own for preferring to believe that basic pupil performance derives from family background instead of school response to family background. Whether or not we will ever effectively teach the children of the poor is probably far more a matter of politics than of social science, and that is as it should be. ... We can, whenever and wherever we choose, successfully teach all students whose schooling is of interest to us. We already know more than we

need to do so. Whether or not we do it must finally depend on how we feel about the fact that we haven't so far."

As odd as this may sound, few individuals in the Brazosport Independent School District were ready to accept the idea that we could teach all children. But, little by little, a new concept had emerged that went something like this: "All children can learn when given the appropriate time and resources. Perhaps not on the same day or in the same way, but all children can learn." Progress.

Over the past 30 years, numerous studies have validated the basic concepts of the effective school. The research has tremendous implications for all educators. Instead of telling us what we can't accomplish, the research tells us *we can all make a difference.* We can no longer remain complacent. Environment, family background, and peer membership are not to blame.

The Effective Schools principles—believing in the ability of all children to learn, the value of the principal as a key instructional leader, and high expectations for success—set new standards. When we see a poor child in the classroom or a student who has recently immigrated, hoping for a better way of life, we can offer him or her a real chance. We can close the gap in student performance. We can change lives.

Coupling the principles and tools of Total Quality Management and the Effective Schools philosophy would be an important step in our effort to close that gap and to change those lives.

Chapter 5

Going Deming's Way

We were off to 2301 Brazosport Boulevard in Freeport, Texas, headquarters of Dow Chemical's Texas operations. In addition to serving as Dow's largest manufacturing site, the complex is home to research and development as well as technical laboratories.

Dow had used the quality approach for years and found it very successful in finding new and improved products and processes for such businesses as plastics, epoxies, hydrocarbons, and chlor/alkali. The company uses TQM throughout its operations, from finding better ways to produce, test, and ship products to providing better customer support to conducting more productive meetings. School board member and Dow employee Joe Bowman believed strongly that some of the same processes and ways of thinking were transferable to education. And, as it turned out, he was right.

Our Dow training began with a short history lesson on the contributions of W. Edwards Deming, considered the father of quality control. We would learn about Deming's practical tools for business success, including his "14 Points" and his famous four-part improvement cycle, called the Plan-Do-Check-Act Cycle. Our assignment was to determine whether or not these methods, which were so helpful to business, could work for us.

W. Edwards Deming came to prominence in the 1950s when the Japanese Union of Science and Engineering (JUSE) turned to the Yale-educated statistician to inject new life into its ailing, post-war economy. This was a time when the label "Made in Japan" did not have a positive connotation.

The Japanese were familiar with the contributions of statisticians like Deming, Joseph M. Juran, and Walter A. Shewhart to America's wartime industry. During World War II, they had taken statistical analysis to a new level by providing practical ways to manage an unskilled labor force and to produce large quantities of high-quality armaments. The resulting effort was called by some "the miracle that won the war."

Leaders of JUSE hoped Dr. Deming might share these methods. They invited him to visit Japan to deliver a series of seminars to the nation's top industrialists that would offer insight and methods for increasing quality and cutting costs.

The Japanese audiences were at first skeptical when Deming told them they could gain dominance in world markets in less than five years—if they adopted his methods. Some even thought the notion impossible. Nevertheless, they were impressed enough to put his ideas into practice. Within six weeks, a number of them began reporting gains of as much as 30 percent without buying new equipment.[1] It wasn't long before virtually all of Japan's major manufacturing plants were employing Deming's methods. Just as he had projected, there was a swift revolution in Japanese manufacturing and a subsequent global demand for Japanese products that continues to this day. In recognition of his friendship and contributions, the highest quality award in Japan was named in Deming's honor. The Deming Prize is still given annually.

It took another 20 years for the "quality" movement to gain momentum on our own shores. Many of the lessons related to quality control had been lost after the close of the war. During the years that followed, U.S. industries experienced a steady decline. Japan was foremost among the competition, having taken advantage of technological advances, new methods of approaching work and the work force, and strengthening its position in global markets. Many U.S. companies now turned to Deming for help—among them Ford Motor Company, Hewlett-Packard, General Motors, AT&T, and Xerox Corporation.

[1]Myron Tribus, "Deming's Way," Massachusetts Institute of Technology, 1981.

Deming's platform at home was no different than in Japan. He would often begin, "Can you blame your competitor for your woes? No. Can you blame the Japanese? No. You did it yourself."[2]

He urged them to monitor the innovations of their competitors, learn from them, and adapt their ideas. This practice is also referred to as "benchmarking." He urged the American companies to shift their focus away from short-term profits and instead to the long-term pursuit of continuous quality improvement. Profits were not a company's true purpose, he said. Rather, a company should seek to provide jobs, stay in business, and create products that enhance the quality of life.[3]

Deming based his Total Quality Management system on "14 Points" that he maintained were essential for business success. To improve quality, productivity, and competitive position, he recommended that companies:

1. create constancy of purpose,
2. adopt the new philosophy (the mission for quality),
3. cease reliance on mass inspection,
4. end the practice of doing business on price alone,
5. improve constantly and forever the system of production and service,
6. institute training on the job,
7. institute leadership,
8. drive out fear,
9. break down barriers between staff areas,
10. eliminate slogans and targets for the work force,
11. eliminate numerical quotas,
12. remove barriers to pride and joy of workmanship,
13. institute a vigorous program of education and retraining, and
14. take action to accomplish the transformation.

[2]*Houston Chronicle,* April 5, 1987.
[3]Robert Cole, "What Was Deming's Real Influence," *Across the Board,* Feb. 1987, p. 49.

Deming also maintained that quality must be continuous. It therefore takes the shape of a circle that is constantly defining and redefining the customers' needs and wants. His Plan-Do-Check-Act Cycle represents a practical approach to process analysis and improvement (Figure 2). It can be used for planning, problem solving, and decision making.

The PDCA Instructional Cycle

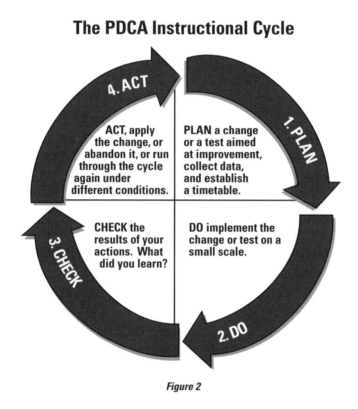

Figure 2

The U.S. company that is most closely associated with Deming's ideas is Ford Motor, for which Deming helped orchestrate a dazzling, if not miraculous, turnaround. Deming signed on as a consultant to Ford in 1980 at a time when the company was about to lose a half billion dollars in a single quarter. His order was tall: to reorganize the entire process by which Ford makes cars. Deming's message of quality, statistical methods, and pride was disseminated throughout all departments—from senior management to assembly line workers. Teams, formed to pool their ideas about improvement, came up with 1,400 suggestions. Of these, 550 were eventually used in the design of two new products, the Taurus and Sable. The addition of these products propelled Ford's sales and profits like never before.[4]

Then CEO Donald E. Petersen summarized Deming's contributions to Ford as follows:

> *In the early 1980s, Dr. Deming did a wonderful job of initiating and agitating the thought processes among a wide array of people at Ford Motor Company. That helped us start the soul-searching and rethinking of how we wanted to function and apply his ideas on quality to our company. All of these discussions ultimately led to our accomplishing the very difficult task of reducing to writing in a simple way the mission, values, and guiding principles that we want the company to operate on. ... The work of Dr. Deming has definitely helped change Ford's corporate leadership. It is management's responsibility to create the environment in which everyone can contribute to continuous improvement in processes and systems. ... Dr. Deming has influenced my thinking in a variety of ways. What stands out is that he helped me crystallize my ideas concerning the value of teamwork, process improvement, and the pervasive power of the concept of continuous improvement.[5]*

Deming's methods and ideas, augmented by others in the quality "movement," eventually led to a great American transformation. More and more leaders in the public and private sector had come to understand that the United States could not maintain and enhance its standard of living in the face of increasing global competition without a new focus on quality. A major effort, spearheaded by C. Jackson Grayson Jr., founder and chairman of the American Productivity & Quality Center (APQC), and Sanford McDonnell, CEO of McDonnell-Douglas, forced public attention on the issue.

---

[4] "Coming Home," *Business Month,* October 1988.
[5] "Deming and the Miracle at Ford," *Business Month,* October 1988.

As a result, the Malcolm Baldrige National Quality Award was created in 1987 as part of the National Quality Improvement Act of 1987 (Public Law 100–107).

Recognizing the critical role that quality plays in the nation's economic growth, the award sought to enhance the competitiveness of U.S. firms through a three-fold mission:

1. promote quality awareness,
2. recognize quality achievement of U.S. businesses, and
3. publicize the prize-winning practices so others can learn from their approach. [6]

Named for the late secretary of commerce, the Baldrige Award was first presented in 1988 by President Ronald Reagan. For its first three years, the award was administered by APQC and the American Society for Quality (ASQ). It is now managed by the Commerce Department's National Institute of Standards and Technology (NIST). Originally created to recognize excellence in manufacturing, service, and small business, the award was expanded in 1999 to include education and healthcare.

Our training at Dow convinced us we needed to change, and now we had the tools to get us there. Our challenge was to integrate Deming's principles with Effective Schools research and apply them to Brazosport. We would begin by asking three questions:

1. Is there enough time to do everything that we want to do and are expected to do in this business?
2. Is there enough money?
3. Are those two things likely to change?

The answers were obvious. No, no, and no. Fortunately, there was still hope. What we needed was focus.

---

[6] *Building on Baldrige: American Quality for the 21st Century*, a publication from the Council on Competitiveness.

We had new ideas and tools that told us we had to be more process-oriented and data-driven. This would help us use the money and the time we had more effectively and more efficiently. And, in this way, we could take our students to higher and higher levels of achievement.

In essence, we were about to change our very culture.

Chapter 6

Designing the Effective, Quality School District

Our TQM training had given us new tools to help manage our time and limited resources. If we could focus and work smarter, we could make Brazosport an effective, quality school district.

Raising Expectations

We realized that our expectations had been too low for too long, especially for children living on the south side of the district. The state had raised its expectations. It told us that all students were expected to pass standards—that is, to demonstrate a certain level of mastery in reading, writing, and mathematics.

Our challenge was never clearer: *We had to teach the kind of student that we had not taught before. And we had to believe that we could.* We were not talking about the kind of students we had successfully taught before or the kind that exists in our dreams. We had to teach *every* child.

It was difficult to admit that we hadn't been doing so all along. Worse yet was the realization that we didn't even have the same high expectations for every student. Patricia Davenport, a member of the management team that attended the Dow training, was one of the first to admit that good intentions had not always served her students well.

As a former teacher and counselor on the south side, Patricia had always worked with at-risk kids. "If anyone had told me that I was not conveying high expectations," she said, "I would have told them to check again." Even though she distributed her questioning patterns evenly across the classroom and respectfully called on each student by his or her first name, Patricia said that the length of time she waited for a response and the kind of encouragement she gave varied. "If I didn't think a child could answer a question correctly, he didn't get much wait time," she explained. "I would say 'OK, John, what is the answer?' After eight seconds, I would turn to Susie on the front row and say, 'Susie, would you help John?' Guess what I did the next day? I called on Susie first. I gave her 83 seconds of wait time and coached her until she had the right answer. Or, if she didn't have it, I didn't ask John to help her. No matter how much I loved all the children, that kind of behavior did not help John or any child in that classroom."

The cornerstone of the Effective Schools philosophy was the belief that we could teach all students. Our eyes had been opened, and we began to ask ourselves some very difficult questions with respect to expectations. These included, "How am I communicating my high/low expectations to my students?" and "Are my expectations different for my high, average, and low achievers?" We began to examine the subtleties of body language and classroom questioning.

An excellent program out of the Los Angeles County Office of Education called Teacher Expectations and Student Achievement (TESA) helped us through this process. It sensitized us to the harmful practices we had used too often when interacting with students. It taught us how to convey high expectations to every child who walks into the classroom. The research is overwhelming: If you believe students can learn and if you set high goals, they will respond accordingly. The TESA program was so enlightening that all teachers and principals in the district were required to take it. (Brazosport continues to offer this training to teachers today.)

We also promote it at seminars throughout the nation. We often start sessions with the tough questions we faced ourselves: "Do you believe that all students can learn? Do you? If you don't, act like you do. You will become convinced. If you can't become convinced, you probably should be doing something else."

Creating a Vision

The TQM training clearly showed us that, to achieve a higher level of performance in our schools, we needed to define what the school district was in business to do. For us, that meant creating a new vision for our district. If done right, it could tell us where we were going and how we would get there. The mission statement had to meet several criteria. It had to be simple, yet compelling. It had to be measurable. And it had to be easily articulated and understood by everyone in the school district.

We knew that the mission statement—no matter how eloquent— could not emanate from the school superintendent, our management group, or any other single department. Its creation had to involve the entire school district. Each member of the organization had to assume ownership of the ideas and translate them into action. If the principals in the schools and the teachers in the classroom weren't part of the process, nothing was going to happen. The real work takes place in the classroom. We drew upon Dow Chemical's Managing Breakthrough process to help us develop a simplified vision, determine realistic objectives, and focus on critical issues.

The first step was to create a positive environment for the free flow of ideas. This involved selecting a team composed of the right size and mix of customers, stakeholders, and employees. In our case, this meant school board members, administrators, principals, teachers, and parents. During brainstorming sessions, we encouraged members to "think outside the box." Teachers were assured that they would not be censored or reprimanded by their principals. Management and outside experts also joined these meetings from time to time to communicate future trends and other information.

To set a framework for our vision, we looked at future trends and asked how we could anticipate their effect on our district. Among the issues raised:

- "What is the area's population projection for the next five years, and what kind of facilities will be needed to handle an increase in enrollment?"
- "What state and federal regulations will go into effect in the next few years, and how must the district comply?"
- "What will wages and budgets look like statewide, and how will that affect our ability to retain and recruit teachers in the future?"

Next, we were asked to "visualize" the district's future. We literally made a picture of how we thought our future might look by cutting magazine photographs and pasting them into a collage. To help with this exercise and the ones that followed, we used a number of quality tools that Dow had shared, including fishbone diagrams and action plans. We used affinity diagrams to identify key elements of the future, relations diagrams to rank the importance of key elements in the future, and pareto charts to illustrate the connections between drivers and results. "Multi voting," another management tool, helped ensure that group members had an equal voice in ranking their ideas.

Michael Abild, Brazosport Independent School District's director of business services, led the quality group facilitation for the district. He was truly masterful at employing the quality tools and facilitating the board and management team to reach consensus.

Finally came the vision statement itself. We needed to develop both a simple vision and supporting objectives. The statement had to be both outcome- and action-oriented. It had to be measurable and tested against the criteria. And leadership would be required to "focus everyone on the new vision." Essentially, that meant that every employee, every parent, every child, and every member of the community would have to adopt it as his or her own.

To draft our statement, we looked at the statements of successful corporations:
- Ford Motor Company: "Quality is Job One"
- The Walt Disney Company: "Making People Happy"
- Toyota Motor Car Corporation: "Building Cars to Love, the World Over"

What single statement could capture all that we wanted to be? After much discussion, we arrived at a vision statement that made us all feel good: "Brazosport Independent School District 2000: An Exemplary School District." But, could it stand up to the test? We evaluated our strengths as well as barriers to achieving the vision. We ranked their importance, as shown in Figure 3.

Strengths and Barriers to Achieving the Vision

STRENGTHS	BARRIERS
• "Exemplary" has positive meaning • Strong tax base • Some campuses are state "exemplary" schools—others are "recognized" • Strong, proven teachers • Improving facilities • Competitive spirit among campuses • Community support • TQM/other planning tools • Good-sized organization • Narrowing focus • Focused, supportive board • Good leadership • Organization in place to accomplish the vision	• State changing accountability system • Different communities in the district (geographical) • Lack of total commitment to accountability • Increased minority populations • Uncertainty in state funding • Exempted populations considered in accountability ratings • Absence of technology plan • Lack of community awareness of accountability ratings • Inconsistent community support • Capacity of schools may inhibit choice • Comfort with status quo

Figure 3

After weighing these, we remained comfortable with our vision and confident that we could achieve it. We now needed to set realistic objectives that had timeframes and were measurable. Each objective would then be categorized into areas or "elements." One of our early 3-year plans for Brazosport ISD resembled the following:

3-5 Year Objectives for Brazosport's Vision

Element: Raise test scores to award-winning levels
Objective:
• By spring 1997, all schools will be "recognized" or "exemplary."

Element: Create an environment that rewards performance
Objective:
• By 1996, develop a local plan to reward campuses rated "recognized" or "exemplary" or "significant improvement" or "sustained high performance" (monetary reward).

Element: Produce graduates who are successful
Objective:
• By 1996–97, develop a survey to determine the success of our graduates (external customer survey).

Element: Increase opportunities for choice
Objectives: • By 1996–97, Brazosport ISD will explore options to allow choice in school attendance.
             • Encourage intelligent choice of dual and concurrent enrollment with community colleges.
             • Develop districtwide tech prep opportunities at Brazosport High School.

Element: Win
Objectives: • Increase awareness of winning by developing criteria for ranking schools compared to each other and to other districts.

Element: Plan
Objectives: • Coordinate planning efforts in the district to ensure consistency of common purposes, goals, vision, etc. (1995–96).
             • Develop vision and strategic plans for district in 1995–96 (goals, targets, etc.).
             • Provide an "adequate" fund balance.
             • Expand site-based budgeting for 1996–97.

Element: Increase parental participation
Objectives: • Raise parents' and community's awareness of performance and goals for improvement (1995–96)
             • Help establish at least one parent teacher organization at each campus (1995–96).

Element: Integrate technology
Objective: • Write proposal for major capital expenditure (1995), gain approval (1995–96), and implement technology plan (1997–98).

Element:	Improve/Add facilities
Objective:	• Pass bond issue (1995–96).
	• Continue refurbishing effort (ongoing).
	• Update demographic study (1995–96).
	• Explore possibility of 5/6 grade school in Clute attendance zone.

We later ranked the objectives in the order of importance and urgency. This helped us determine annual objectives.

We would now turn to Deming's Plan-Do-Check-Act Cycle to help us implement annual goals, stay on course, and review progress throughout the year.

Chapter 7

Looking Within for Hidden Treasure

E ven with a new vision statement and objectives in hand, we were not yet ready to turn to our principals and say, "Here are your goals. Have a good year."

For direction, we again drew upon our TQM training—in this case, the use of best practices. The district's TAAS data, broken out by student, by classroom teacher, and by school, had been revealing. We were finding a number of teachers on both the district's south and north sides whose students scored high on the TAAS. Perhaps more surprisingly, we identified some teachers in the more affluent areas whose economically disadvantaged students scored poorly.

When we looked more closely at the data from the poorer schools, one teacher, in particular, stood out. Her name was Mary Barksdale. Something different was happening in Mary's third-grade classes. Despite the fact that 94 percent of her students were considered "at-risk," virtually all of them had mastered each section of the TAAS.

What was Mary doing differently in her classroom?

Despite her claim that she was "simply teaching," on closer inspection we found that her common-sense approach was a dynamic process of continuous assessment and re-teaching for those students not up to mastery. When Mary's students missed questions on their tests, she didn't see it as a failure on their part. Instead, she set out to determine what part of her instruction had not come across. She then found the time to re-teach that section before moving on to the next chapter. The process had enabled all of her students to excel.

Creating the Eight-Step Process

We later compared Mary's approach to that of other teachers who also were successful teaching at-risk students. There were many features in common. Mary's system, which eventually became known as the Eight-Step Process, is similar to Deming's Plan, Do, Check, Act cycle, but with a twist: It was developed by Mary herself from practices already working in the classroom (Figure 4).

The Eight-Step Process is a data-driven, cyclical continuous improvement approach. While we describe these steps briefly in the following paragraphs, Section II of this book provides an in-depth overview of the PDCA Instructional Cycle, which evolved from the Eight-Step Process and incorporates other best practices.

Step 1: Test Score Disaggregation (Plan). Data taken from the criterion-referenced state assessment scores help chart a course, telling us where we are presently and where we need to be. Teachers begin by reviewing the scores from both their own classes as well as from incoming classes. Teacher teams, formed by grade level or subject area, analyze the data to determine which content areas—and even subskills within these areas—are causing students the most difficulty. Priorities are recorded on a form that ranks skill mastery in these areas from weakest to strongest. The form then serves as both a guide, indicating which areas will need additional classroom attention, as well as a goal-setting document, projecting desired improvements for the coming year.

Step 2: Time Line Development (Plan). Once priorities are established, the same teacher teams create an instructional calendar to address the needs, which puts the most emphasis on those areas where the greatest number of students were shown to need the most help. These calendars, created before the school year begins, outline weekly objectives for the year and are shared throughout the school. Because colleagues work on the same curriculum each week of the semester, there is ample opportunity for continued collaboration after class to work through common problems. Even teachers in other disciplines help reinforce the week's objectives, working together to meet the school's academic goals.

Step 3: Instructional Focus (Do). Teachers are now ready to cover the instructional objectives and target areas as scheduled. The district

The Eight-Step Process

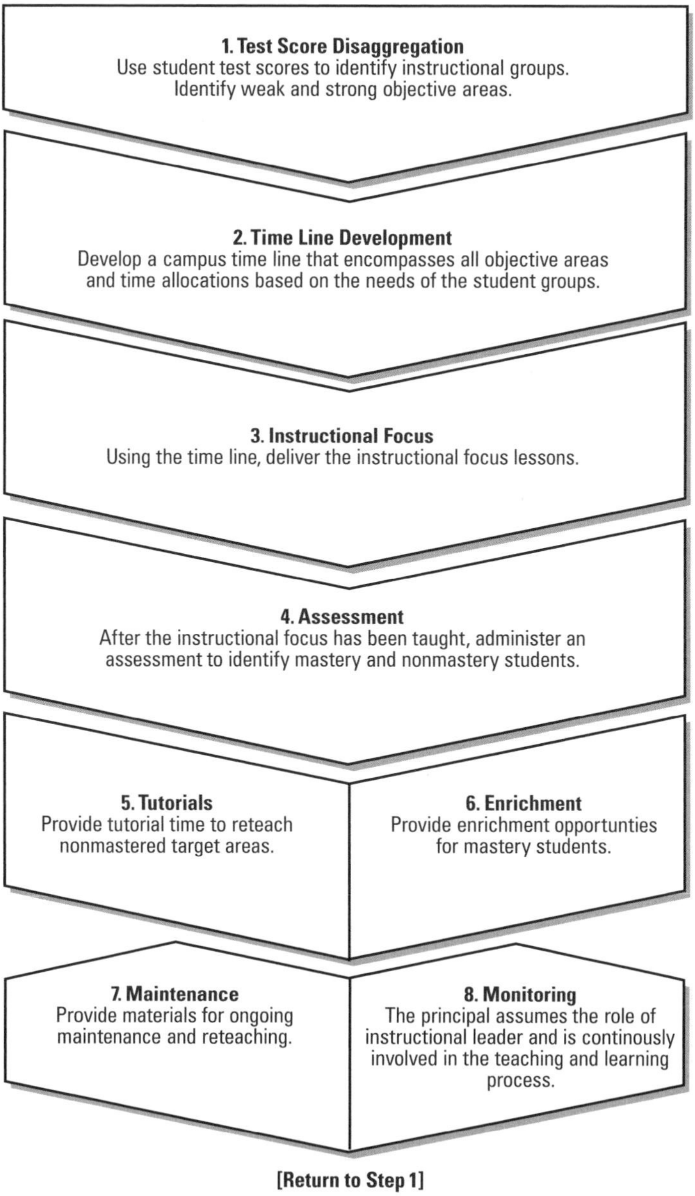

1. Test Score Disaggregation
Use student test scores to identify instructional groups.
Identify weak and strong objective areas.

2. Time Line Development
Develop a campus time line that encompasses all objective areas
and time allocations based on the needs of the student groups.

3. Instructional Focus
Using the time line, deliver the instructional focus lessons.

4. Assessment
After the instructional focus has been taught, administer an
assessment to identify mastery and nonmastery students.

5. Tutorials
Provide tutorial time to reteach
nonmastered target areas.

6. Enrichment
Provide enrichment opportunties
for mastery students.

7. Maintenance
Provide materials for ongoing
maintenance and reteaching.

8. Monitoring
The principal assumes the role of
instructional leader and is continously
involved in the teaching and learning
process.

[Return to Step 1]

Figure 4

provides a "Lesson Bank" containing detailed information on teaching strategies that have proved effective in the past for each objective on the calendar. While the instructional focus is mandatory, teachers retain flexibility in delivering the content. They may choose to use their own methods or may draw upon the resources of the Lesson Bank.

Step 4: Assessment (Check). At the end of each instructional unit, tests are administered to identify mastery and nonmastery students. These tests are ready-made, collectively administered by grade level (elementary) or subject area (middle and upper level), and normally have only four questions. The idea is to use a brief, focused assessment and to test frequently. In this way, teachers learn right away whether the majority of students have grasped the content or if more time needs to be devoted to a particular unit. Generally, if 80 percent or more of the students completed at least three of the four questions accurately, the class moves on.

Steps 5 and 6: Tutorials and Enrichment (Act). Each day, a 30- to 60-minute "team time" is set aside as an elective. Assessment results determine whether a student will spend team time in a "tutorial" or an "enrichment" period. While tutorials are for review and refocus, they are treated in a positive light and as a way for students to catch up.

Students not requiring additional focus are assigned to enrichment periods, where they may choose from a list of electives or enrichment courses. Because they understand that their TAAS performance dictates which program they will enter, students actually work harder during the regular class period to master objectives. In this way, individuals who might normally slack off pay closer attention in regular class and reap the rewards. Even students who begin the year in the tutorial team time often earn the right to move into the enrichment period.

Step 7: Maintenance (Check). Because we all tend to forget skills over time, formal reviews are scheduled throughout the calendar year. These intensify before the TAAS tests are administered. Teachers understand that this is an important time to reinforce concepts and skills. They draw lessons from approved "maintenance" guidelines and are encouraged to model skills and thought processes in lively, interactive sessions.

Step 8. Monitoring (Check). The principal assumes the lead role in monitoring classroom and schoolwide progress. This involves regular classroom visits as well as meetings with individual teachers, teacher teams, and individual students. The process ensures that priorities remain clear and the school's academic mission stays on focus.

After the Eight-Step Process was drafted and refined, Mary Barksdale and Principal Sam Williams implemented the process at Velasco Elementary. Known as the lowest-performing school in the district, Velasco had the highest number (85 percent) of students who qualified for the federal lunch program and the lowest test scores among Brazosport schools. Some of its students' TAAS scores were in the single-digit percentile rankings. The school had already been tagged by the Texas Education Agency as "Accredited/Warned," which had put the school on notice for possible state involvement.

Why did we start with Velasco? We thought if they could improve student performance there, then other campuses with fewer numbers of poor children would have no excuse for not trying to improve. The goal was for Velasco to become a "recognized" or "exemplary" campus. And while the school didn't make it to that level the first year, tremendous improvements were made, earning Velasco a "significant gains" award from the Texas Education Agency.

What had Velasco done that worked so well? Teachers used the Eight-Step Process as well as other systems for improvement to become data- driven and focused. They eliminated subjectivity and instead began to systemically identify subject areas that needed more instruction as well as students who needed more help. To prepare students for tests, they drilled the subject matter again and again. And, after testing, they revisited the concepts that were missed.

"We also had to revamp our homework policy and testing policy to account for poverty and a nonsupportive home life," Sam Williams added.

He said that because many students didn't have supportive parents or a place or time to do homework, tutorial sites were established at neighborhood churches, youth homes, and apartment complexes. "We needed to help the kids outside of school and outside of their homes."

There was more. Mary, Sam, and the teachers of Velasco got to know each student on a personal level, meeting one on one to plan personal activities that would help them master standards. In the process they conveyed high expectations. "Consistent high expectations are a must," Mary Barksdale explained. "If students know what is expected, they will deliver. I have never met a student who truly does not want to learn."

After school and on weekends, Sam, Mary, and teachers met to develop and update the instructional focus and calendar, monitor progress, and assess results. Brainstorming sessions allowed teachers to share ideas on what was working in their classrooms that might be replicated in others.

Importantly, everyone began sharing ideas and working together:
- student and teacher,
- instructional coordinator and teacher,
- instructional coordinator and principal,
- principal and student, and
- superintendent and principal.

The following year, we asked Mary to serve full-time as TAAS coordinator both at Velasco Elementary and Fleming Elementary, another school on the district's south side.

Clara Sale-Davis, principal at Fleming at the time, remembers that improvements went beyond curriculum and instruction to creating a better, safer environment. "Gangs were a big problem, with graffiti and violence on campus," she said. "We turned it (around) by having the Crips and the Bloods call a truce on campus, declaring it a nonviolent zone." She explained that the school dealt harshly with fighting infractions by providing a police citation and automatic five-day assignment to an alternative placement center.

By implementing the Eight Steps and improving them along the way, the faculty and students responded well. Expanded areas of emphasis included consistency in delivery of instruction, building on the strengths of others, common planning time, and modeling effective teaching behaviors. For their efforts, both Velasco and

Fleming received a "recognized" rating at the end of the year. And Velasco became the first campus in the district with more than 50 percent of its students in the "economically disadvantaged" category to receive this rating.

The following year, we asked Mary to take on a similar role at each of the district's south-side schools—Brazosport High School, Freeport Intermediate, Lanier Middle School, as well as Velasco and Fleming.

At first, the idea of using a new teaching method was not warmly received, especially at Brazosport High. After introducing Mary and the Eight-Step Process, some of the faculty members looked at us in amazement. One of them asked, "You expect us to take time out of our regular curriculum to teach kids how to read, write, and do math?" We replied, "Think about what you have just said. How can students do your regular curriculum if they can't read, write, and do mathematics?"

"It was not easy," Mary recalls. "Change is hard, and most of us resist change. Principals and teachers, especially at the secondary level, were not especially receptive to an elementary teacher advising them on what to teach, the delivery of instruction, or when to teach a skill."

Yes, there was resistance. There was skepticism. There were failures. Some made excuses; they did not believe then that "all students can learn." But they adjusted, and with persistence, vision, hard work, and leadership, the Eight Steps began to work in these schools too.

When given clear evidence that another teacher's methods could win them superior results, these teachers became the program's most vociferous advocates. By the end of the year, all five schools received a "recognized" or "exemplary" rating, and Brazosport ISD received a "recognized" rating as well.

Principals from other campuses were now coming to us; they didn't want their schools left out. Thus, we began replicating the process throughout the district. By the 1996–97 academic year, all of the Brazosport schools had adapted the Eight Steps to suit the needs of their campuses and students. And, by year's end, 17 of our 18 campuses had achieved either "recognized" or "exemplary" status.

This was quite an accomplishment considering that only five years earlier nine of these schools had been labeled "low performing." (Interestingly, the only school that did not make the grade was in Lake Jackson, a school with fewer than 10 percent poor students. Not without a little embarrassment and parent encouragement, that school skipped "recognized" and went straight on to become "exemplary" the following year.)

In 1997–98, all 18 of our campuses were classified as either "recognized" or "exemplary." All student groups had demonstrated a subject mastery of 90 percent or better. We had become an exemplary school district two years ahead of our vision statement target. We did it again in 1998-99.

For its accomplishments, the Quality Texas Foundation selected Brazosport Independent School District, along with a division of Dell Computer Corporation of Austin and TDIndustries of Dallas, to receive the prestigious 1998 Texas Quality Award. Patterned after the Malcolm Baldrige National Quality Award, the honor recognizes organizations that are role models for quality, customer satisfaction, and performance excellence in Texas.

In announcing the winners of the 1998 award, Rick Thrasher, executive director of the Texas Department of Economic Development, said, "We are delighted that, for the first time, one of the recipients is a public education institution. It is impossible to grow our economy without an educated work force. Brazosport Independent School District, Dell Computer Corporation, and TDIndustries are outstanding examples of the kinds of organizations that are causing Texas to lead the nation in economic growth."

The following year, Brazosport ISD became a finalist in the education category of the 1999 Malcolm Baldrige Quality Award, along with the Hunterdon Central Regional High School in New Jersey. While neither educational institution won the award, it is considered an honor to receive a site visit by a Malcolm Baldrige Quality Award team.

Texas Education Agency Commissioner Jim Nelson described the district's remarkable transformation in a recent interview:

> *The significant improvement in student performance in Brazosport Independent School District is a testament to the district's strong leadership as well as the hard work of its dedicated students and teachers. It is an example of the great things that can be accomplished when educators commit themselves to education reform. Instead of making excuses for inadequate student performance, Brazosport Independent School District rose to meet the challenges placed on the district by the state's accountability system. The result was unprecedented academic success in the district.*

The time had come to take our vision statement to a higher level. It became "BISD: Exemplary and Beyond." We now wanted each campus to be "exemplary," with at least 90 percent of its students mastering state standards. But we wanted to go beyond TAAS as the only measurement of our success.

We now set a target of having at least 90 percent of all student groups—African American, Hispanic, white, economically disadvantaged—scoring 1,000 or better on the SAT. Another objective was greater student enrollment in advanced placement and the Globe Scholars programs, each offering a more rigorous curriculum. Placement of junior and senior high students in classes at the community college became another high priority. Here, students could earn both high school and college credit at the same time; a few graduated from our local community college the second week of May and from the local high school two weeks later.

We had gone from excuses to results. Our journey began with a state mandate that said no student would get a diploma without learning standards. The school board's jump-start provided impetus and resources. Superintendent Gerald Anderson provided the leadership that made things happen. Patricia Davenport coordinated the process and made the connections between each campus. Mary Barksdale served as role model and mentor. Sam Williams and the principals who followed provided campus leadership. But the actual work—the teaching—went on in the classroom. The teachers were the ones who got the job done.

Chapter References

"Brazosport Independent School District, Erasing the Achievement Gap," *The Results Fieldbook*, Mike Schmoker, Association for Supervision and Curriculum Development, Alexandria, Va., 2001.

Interviews with Clara Sale-Davis and Sam Williams for APQC Baldrige in Education Initiative, May 11, 1999.

Interview with Jim Nelson, Texas Education Commissioner, October 24, 2001.

Notes from Mary Dunbar Barksdale's draft book, *Educate*, as shared with Jack Grayson, American Productivity & Quality Center, February 2000.

Rick Thrasher quote excerpted from the Quality Texas Foundation press release, May 5, 1998, http://www.texas-quality.org/98winners.html.

Part II:

The PDCA Instructional Cycle

Part II

The PDCA Instructional Cycle

P atricia Davenport and Gerald Anderson left the Brazosport Independent School District in 2000 to pursue a shared mission of closing the achievement gap at other school districts across the nation. Patricia works with the Education Initiative of the American Productivity & Quality Center and serves as a private educational consultant. Gerald also is an independent consultant. Both provide their expertise at numerous seminars and conferences sponsored primarily by APQC, the National School Conference Institute (NSCI), and other educational organizations, in addition to providing training to individual schools and school districts nationally.

The authors firmly believe the Brazosport experience is transferable and that other school districts can also enjoy vast improvements by adopting quality principles and Effective Schools tenets. The Eight Steps used in Brazosport is just one example of a successful quality process. In the chapters that follow, the authors introduce the PDCA Instructional Cycle, a quality framework for planning, administration, and vision setting based on the Deming/Shewhart/PDCA model (Figure 5, page 60).

The PDCA Instructional Cycle blends Brazosport's Eight Steps with quality principles and Effective Schools research. It stresses the use of quality tools throughout the system and the importance of involving every employee.

The authors invite other districts to consider using use this Plan-Do-Check-Act cycle as a basis for designing a program that meets their particular needs. Section II provides their recipe for how to do it.

PDCA Instructional Cycle

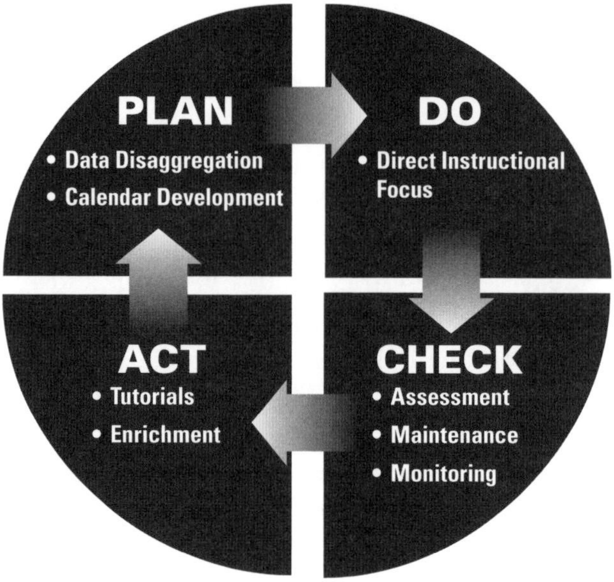

Figure 5

Chapter 8

PLAN
Data Disaggregation

"Disaggregation is a practical, hands-on process that allows a school's faculty to answer two critical questions: 'Effective at what? Effective for whom?' It is not a problem-solving process but a problem-finding process."
—Lezotte and Jacoby, Sustainable School Reform

Before Brazosport Independent School District set its objectives to improve student achievement, its faculty members already had an abundance of data available to them, but they had little knowledge of how to use it to their advantage. Teachers and administrators rarely analyzed the results of standardized tests, and there was little talk of how these tests could be used to improve instruction. The Texas Education Agency's requirement that student TAAS results be "disaggregated" and then published provided the impetus to change this.

Today, as a result of the Brazosport experience, people are looking at the data before acting out of prejudice or ignorance. Data disaggregation—defined as dividing the data into its constituent parts—is the critical first step of the PDCA Instructional Cycle and essential to the planning process. It allows administrators and teachers to base their planning and instructional decisions on fact, diagnose problems, and work together to close gaps in student achievement. Data is never used to punish, only to point the way to success.

Have a Vision In Place First

Disaggregation is a powerful driver for positive change. Remember what happened when the results of the TAAS tests were made public in Brazosport? Data was the vehicle that helped the district, its schools, and its teachers evaluate their effectiveness. It made them see the need for change.

Data disaggregation can be a catalyst for action. When creating a new vision for its district, Brazosport personnel used data to assess existing conditions and determine what patterns, practices, and operating procedures were enhancing or impeding their vision. That information was critical in preparing their vision and objectives and executing their plan of action.

When creating a vision for your district, conduct an analysis to determine whether or not the curriculum is being equitably learned by all students. Use data disaggregation as a benchmark to:

- determine what percentage of students are mastering the essentials at each grade level (by program, course, school, and teacher) and
- determine whether the various subgroups—socioeconomic, race, and gender—are mastering the essentials to the same degree.

Once you have analyzed where your district is, obtain consensus for where you want to be in the coming years and how you will get there. Ask these questions:

- How will students benefit if the vision is achieved?
- What is the planning process that will guide the vision?
- What opportunities will people have to learn?
- How will we monitor progress?
- Will achieving the vision make a positive difference?
- What are the strengths and barriers with regard to achieving the mission?
- Are our objectives and timeframe realistic and measurable?

Involve the right mix of stakeholders in your planning sessions and provide sufficient time and resources to create a clear vision, objectives, and goals. (Refer to Chapter 6 for ideas on creating a vision.) Also, consider partnering with nearby companies; invite them to share quality tools that have worked for them. Remember that Dow Chemical's Managing Breakthrough Process served as the basis for designing Brazosport's vision (Figure 6).

Managing Breakthough Process

```
                    ┌─────────────────┐
                    │  District Vision │
                    └────────┬────────┘
                             │
   ┌──────────────┐  ┌──────────────┐      ┌──────────────┐
   │ Vision Element│──│ Vision Element│──────│ Vision Element│
   └──────┬───────┘  └──────────────┘      └──────────────┘
          │
   ┌──────────────┐
   │ Objectives (Goals)│
   └──────┬───────┘
          │
   ┌──────────────┐
   │ Annual Objectives│
   └──────┬───────┘
          │
   ┌──────────────┐
   │ Implementation │
   │     Plans      │
   └──────┬───────┘
          │
   ┌──────────┴──────────┐
┌──────────────┐  ┌──────────────┐
│Periodic Reviews│  │    P D C A    │
└──────────────┘  └──────────────┘
```

Figure 6

Using Data to Identify Opportunities for Improvement

Once your vision is in place at the district level, implement the plan at the school and classroom level. Here's what to do:

- Disaggregate your data (standards test results) by school, by grade, by class, by teacher, by student, by socioeconomic status, and even by question.
- Disaggregate the data by additional outcome indicators, such as attendance, dropout rate, extracurricular participation, graduation rate, grade distribution, honors earned, retention, suspensions, truancy, and vandalism.
- Distribute reports showing the data breakdown to every elementary, middle, and high school teacher in the district. (Before reviewing these reports, provide every administrator and teacher with special training in data interpretation.)
- Analyze the data. What conclusions can be drawn about the equity of student outcomes? How effective is the school in teaching all students? How effective is the school in teaching core

subject areas such as reading, writing, and math? Why do the results look the way they do?

- Hold teachers and administrators accountable for improvements.

Data disaggregation may tell us, for example, whether most fifth graders, in general, need additional time on fractions or if only Kate and John need additional practice. On a broader level, disaggregation points out trends where additional emphasis is required. When this happens, teachers can be asked to align the curriculum to meet specific needs. For example, fifth grade teachers may observe that their students as well as the preceding third and fourth grade classes are consistently missing questions on synonyms and antonyms. In this case, the fifth grade teachers share this data with the third and fourth grade teachers. Together they develop lessons that will reinforce these skills in each of their classes. In this way, introduction of the concept and practice in the earlier grades help prepare students for material to come. Each new school year builds upon the previous one, beginning with kindergarten and ending with grade 12.

How does this apply to kindergarten through second grade teachers when their students aren't tested until third grade? Until Brazosport started analyzing the TAAS data, the district's leaders didn't really understand the relationship between results for grades three through five and the foundation years' efforts. On TAAS test days, K–2 teachers brought in cookies and balloons with notes for grades 3–5 teachers that basically said, "Good luck, we are with you all the way." In truth, the K–2 teachers were probably relieved that their students weren't being tested.

After a few years, the third grade teachers realized that K–2 teachers could do much more than bake cookies and that, in fact, their efforts were determining the fate of third grade scores. The kindergarten teachers were asked to review the older students' TAAS data, note which concepts students were consistently missing, and introduce and reinforce these in their classrooms. Today, first and second grade teachers receive a copy of the third grade calendar. When a main idea is introduced to third graders for three weeks in October, that concept is simultaneously introduced at the earlier grades for the same three-week period. As a result, third grade scores have risen. (More about calendar development in the next chapter.)

Academic Groupings

Brazosport also uses data disaggregation to organize student groups by academic performance. Dr. Shirley Crook, who came into the district early on to teach us how to disaggregate and use our data to improve instruction, devised five groupings (Figure 7) to describe a child's level of proficiency. Brazosport uses these groupings to communicate a student's mastery so that other teachers may quickly discover where help is needed.

How is this information used? Let's say Johnny is transferring to another school in the district. His current teacher might call his new

Proficiency Groupings

Instructional Group	Description
Mastery students	Students who performed exceptionally in every testing area
System students	Students who just missed the test objective or mastery standard
Bubble students	Students who need to work in specific skill areas and are candidates for tutoring
Reteach students	Students who did not grasp the material and need intensive remedial instruction (Investigate whether the teaching method used could be a contributing factor.)
Foundation students	Students who may be identified as eligible for special education

Figure 7

teacher to say: "Johnny is leaving my class today and will be attending your class on Monday. Please be aware that Johnny is a mastery student in reading and language; he is a bubble student in math." The new teacher has immediate information from which to ease Johnny's transition into the classroom. Similarly, a student's current teacher may use these descriptions when conferring with his teacher from the previous year. The teachers feel comfortable using these references because everyone knows what they mean. Similarly, transfer students from out-of-state schools are required to take diagnostic tests in the core curricular areas in order to determine what their academic grouping and subsequent placement will be.

We recommend that you create similar groupings for your districts. They are strictly used for teacher reference. When students walk into the classroom for the first time, teachers have a common vocabulary that helps them assess where each child stands academically and where concentration should be made in class. It helps us do a better job.

Teacher Teams

Looking at the data as a team is at the heart of the improvement process. We recommend that your district form teacher teams or "quality teams" to analyze data by grade level or subject area. Challenge them to devise lesson plans that raise student performance. Such a team might consist of the special education teacher, all fourth grade teachers, the Title 1 coordinator, the math specialist, and the state assessment coordinator. Teachers outside the state assessment areas such as art, music, physical education, and media resources as well as librarians, counselors, and special education teachers should also be invited.

At Brazosport, everyone was expected to collaborate, and there was no tolerance for "I am in physical education, so I am not responsible for this." In addition to collaboration by grade level and subject area, teams may form to address concerns regarding individual student groups, ethnicity, gender, or socioeconomic status.

This approach is a shift from the old paradigm of "one teacher and his/her students" to groups of teachers with responsibility for an entire grade level or subject area. The old approach tended to blame the students for unacceptable scores—"What's wrong with those kids? I know I taught them that standard." The team approach helps us look at student scores in relation to teacher performance, to accept the results, and to work to resolve problems—"Apparently they didn't get it; what should we do differently this year?"

At Brazosport, TAAS testing occurs in late April, and the results are normally available before the school year begins. This allows the teams to get a heads up on the school year and use the data to note where students are grasping concepts or missing them and plan the next year's instructional calendar accordingly. Teams also share ideas on how to do things differently—perhaps adjusting the curriculum, textbook, or strategy. In our experience, teachers will almost always embrace proven methods that enable their students to succeed.

A Case Example

| WEAK/STRONG OBJECTIVES: | Math | GRADE 3 | FOR GRADE 4 |

Arrange from weakest objective to strongest objective

% Passing: 94

% Passing		Objective	
52	Objective 4	–	Measurement
52	Objective 12	–	Mathematical Representation
53	Objective 11	–	Solution Strategies
56	Objective 7	–	Subtraction
60	Objective 10/13	–	Estimation/Reasonable Need
66	Objective 2	–	Algebraic Concepts
68	Objective 1	–	Number Concepts

Figure 8

Ample collaboration time—as much as 70 minutes a day—should be allotted for quality team planning. During these meetings, members can analyze their students' performance across the board and determine what they can do collectively to improve teachers' performance. Together they create meaningful lesson plans that are interrelated and aligned to the TAAS standards. The sessions also provide time to determine how to structure classes and when to divide students into groups that 1) need additional time for review and testing or 2) will use that time for enrichment activities.

Where do you find the extra time to hold these meetings? Instead of letting the schedule run you, schedule your day—from beginning to end—to accommodate student needs. For example, 30 minutes can be added every day by taking three to four minutes off each class period. You go to the special education teacher and say, "Would you like your students a little longer on Fridays so we can have common planning times, and we will keep them a little longer Monday through Thursday?" Or, you might go in 30 minutes early on Wednesdays and Fridays and meet by grade level.

The point is that only you know what your students need. Therefore, use the data and experience to convince the principal, the director of curriculum, or whomever that you need more time for planning, tutorials, or other activities. When your arguments are convincing, leaders/decision makers usually agree that changing the schedule or providing additional resources can help achieve the desired result. At Brazosport, we kept this thought in mind at all times: It is far more important to make our schedule meet the needs of our students than to fit the kids to the schedule so the buses run on time.

Talking with the 'Client'

One of the most important and rewarding things you can do with the data is to plan a one-on-one review with all students, the "customers," to help them understand their progress. We have been amazed at what happens when we start treating our students as the primary stakeholders.

At Brazosport, we provided two opportunities for what we call Test Talks. Students first meet with the principal or assistant principal and later with their teacher. The student receives an appointment slip for Principal Test Talk and brings it to his teacher—"Excuse me, Miss Smith, I have an appointment with the principal." Students love being singled out in this important way.

The principal talks about the student's academic achievement, discussing those areas to celebrate as well as areas where extra care is needed. The principal is painstakingly clear about those areas where attention and improvement are necessary. "This area is yellow, which means 'caution,' so slow down. You need to be careful," he or she might say. "This hot pink marker is a 'stop and pay attention' zone. You did not master this standard. I know you can do better here.

Your teacher knows it, I know it, and you know it. You need to pay very close attention when your teacher covers this in class."

This message, communicated in an upbeat, though authoritative manner, comes through time after time. At the end of the appointment, the child gets a sticker that says, "I had a Principal Test Talk." The child selects a piece of candy and goes back to class. It has been a positive experience that will be repeated again with the child's teacher (even the candy). Both talks serve to motivate and reward students, and equally as important, to secure the student's own commitment to succeed.

When we began Test Talks, we offered it only to "at-risk" children. Brazosport now conducts them with every single child. Parents are not invited. We found that they often didn't show up or, if they did, they tended to take over the session: "What? Kate failed multiplication!? She knows her threes—go ahead and recite your threes." We hold a separate Parent Test Talk in the evening. If a parent doesn't show up there, it is not an embarrassment to the child.

One of the great benefits of the Test Talk is that it tells every child, "Your academic success is important to me, because I care about you as a person." This can be a powerful moment in the life of a child, and it can change a young life forever.

When we really get to know our students and start talking to them about their educational achievement, they become more serious about testing. Because they know that academic decisions are based on test results, they do their best. Ultimately, they take ownership of the process and become responsible for their own learning.

Academic Teams, Too

Another planning strategy that worked well at Brazosport schools was the creation of classroom academic teams.

Students consider themselves part of a team. They celebrate when the entire class does well on state assessments and other group activities. They collaborate, help each other, and share in each others' successes. As the year progresses, students who are not meeting academic or behavior expectations are reminded that they are letting down not only themselves but the other members of the team.

The concept encourages students to do their best. Teams are rewarded for performance excellence with coupons for soft drinks, food, movie passes, and other treats.

One elementary school in the district carries the team concept even farther. Like a football draft, faculty members hand pick their academic team for the forthcoming year. An index card, created for each student, lists the student's name, recent standardized test data, and other information related to strengths and weaknesses. The teachers choose their students in draft style and agree not to disclose the order in which they made their selections. When school begins, the teachers inform their classes that they chose each and every one of them. Parents are also informed of the selection and are generally pleased that their child was personally selected, rather than randomly placed in a classroom by a computer. (Other schools in the district use more traditional methods for class selection.)

The point is that learning can be fun and the rewards plentiful when everyone is a winner.

Chapter Reference

Lawrence W. Lezotte and Barbara C. Jacoby, *Sustainable School Reform: The District Context for School Improvement;* Effective Schools Products, Ltd.; 1992.

Chapter 9

PLAN
Calendar Development

*"What you do on the first days of school will determine
your success or failure for the rest of the school year. You will either
win or lose your class on the first days of school."*
—*Harry Wong*

Larry Lezotte once wrote that one of the best kept secrets in education is that students will learn what we teach them. Educators who understand this and who manage their classroom time wisely can accomplish almost anything.

As discussed in the last chapter, we recommend that teachers meet together long before the academic year begins to build in-depth instructional calendars. The challenge is to determine how much time needs to be allotted to cover the priority objectives identified during the data analysis. The goal is to get each child up to standards. To make decisions, teachers must ask themselves:

• What do students need to know?
• What do I need to teach?
• How much time do I need to do it?

The calendar is created in response to these questions by placing the instructional focus squarely where attention is needed the most. Once completed, the calendar is shared across the entire campus and integrated into every teacher's instructional framework. Every staff member—no matter whether career counselor, technology advisor, physical education instructor, or school nurse—checks with the calendar to reinforce concepts that will be studied that period.

For example, if the third grade teachers are working on geometric shapes, the third grade art teacher may have her classes make them in art. Likewise, the kindergarten, first grade, and second grade teachers can also incorporate geometric shapes into their lesson plans.

Similarly, at a higher grade level, the physical education teacher doesn't simply have the class run the 50-yard dash. Instead, she checks the instructional calendar and notes that math teachers will be working on estimation and bar graphing. To support these objectives, she asks her students to jot down their estimated time on the dash, then record their actual times and create a bar graph that shows the difference. In this way, we get two rewards: first, students work on mastering the objectives, and second, they learn that estimation and bar graphing have real-world applications outside of class.

The calendar is a work in progress. Depending on the needs of the students and the weight of the objective, the calendar should:

- be adjusted to allow more or less time to cover a target area;
- cover each of the standards on the state assessment, with additional time for those areas where students are having the most trouble; and
- follow the 80/20 rule in Quality Management, which says that if you focus on the top 20 percent of your weaker objectives all year long, you will get 80 percent of your results back. While the teacher may cover every standard, he or she continually focuses on, for example, comprehension in reading classes and problem solving in math if those were the standards where students were weakest.

The instructional calendar is not your lesson plan or scope and sequence. It is simply a guide that tells teachers what objectives will be taught during a particular week. It ensures us that every concept on the state assessment will be covered in the classroom. It helps align the written curriculum, with the taught curriculum, with the tested curriculum.

Why is this so important? It is simply not fair to expose students to problems or test them on material for which they have had no preparation. It sets them up for failure. One year we reviewed our data for fourth graders and found that they had scored the lowest on "inference." When we did some checking, we found that we hadn't taught inference until May, a month after the test was administered. Whose fault was it? It certainly was not the students' focus. The point is that using common sense is essential when planning the calendar.

The calendar also is a great time-management tool. It gets us started on the first day of school and keeps us focused throughout the year. Before Brazosport used the calendar, a significant amount of time was lost. Between August 10 and Labor Day, there was no serious instruction in the classroom. We spent too much time covering textbooks, talking about family vacations, reviewing classroom rules, and signing up for the lunch program. We got into gear about the middle of September and worked hard until Thanksgiving. Then it was time off for holiday plays and other festivities. The students were hyped, so we really didn't think we could accomplish much until after New Year's. Then it was back to work, but ... oh, thank goodness, for spring break. Then spring itself. Before you knew it, another year had come and gone.

That was before standards. Brazosport faculty members now know how important each day is and take advantage of every instructional moment available. After marking out holiday and staff development days, they were amazed at how few days they actually had to teach.

Today, a fourth grade teacher immediately gets her class on track in August with, "Welcome to my class. We are going to have a great year." She then spends at least 10 minutes that same day focusing on the calendar's "main ideas" related to reading. Then the first reading lesson begins. With the calendar to help keep pace, instruction stays on focus—even between Thanksgiving and New Year's and the first and last weeks of school.

Bringing Parents On Board

The calendar belongs to everybody. We have found it most beneficial to meet with parents and explain why we use the calendar and how important it is for their child's achievement. In these meetings, we explain the state standards that students are expected to master by the year's end. We then hand them a calendar and say, "We are sharing our calendar with you to let you know what standards we are emphasizing during a particular timeframe. We want to make sure your child learns these standards. Your help at home would be great!"

Occasionally we run up against a parent who believes that standards "dumb down" the curriculum. Our usual response to objections of this nature is to sit with these parents to discuss their concerns. We bring out the state standards for that grade, and say, "Let's go through these together and, when we come across one you don't want your child to know, let me know and I will mark it off." So far, we haven't had any takers. Parents who may have been under the impression that standards were low are generally quite impressed with the rigor of the standards established by the state accountability system.

Approaches to Calendar Development

There are a number of approaches to instructional calendar development. Your teams may wish to do the following:

- Divide the number of standards into the number of instructional days between the opening day of school and the testing day to allocate an equal amount of time to each standard. This works well for a grade level whose objective mastery scores changed little from the previous year.
- Schedule the order of standards taught from "weakest to strongest" and concentrate in areas where students are having the greatest difficulty and then moving to areas more easily mastered. Do this from the first day of school until winter break, then administer a practice test and develop a new calendar for the spring semester based on the test results.
- Follow the same procedure as above, but start at the beginning of the school year and complete the process right before the standards test is administered in the spring. In that way, more time is devoted to the objectives the students have the most difficulty mastering.

Although these approaches differ, each can be effective when the calendar is created by the teachers who will be using it and if decisions are based on student data (figures 9 and 10).

A Case Example for Reading

Sun	Mon	Tue	Wed	Thurs	Fri	Sat
Irregular word: **though**	Continuous Reading Focus: Objective 5 ~ 2 *** Integrate Reading Objectives 1–6** Continue reviewing all writing objectives		3	4	5 **Assessment Reading Objective. 5A, 5B, and 5C**	6
7 Irregular word: **thumb**	Begin Reading Focus: Objective 6 ~ 9 *** Integrate Reading Objectives 1–6** Continue reviewing all writing objectives		10	11	12	13
14 Irregular word: **tough**	15 Holiday President's Day	16 **Staff Development Day**	Continuous Reading Focus: 18 Objective 8 ~ *Integrate Reading Objectives 1–8 **Review for TAAS Writing**		19	20
21 Review Irregular words	22 **Review for TAAS Writing Test**	23 **TAAS Writing Test**	24 Continuous Reading Focus: Objective 6 ~ *** Integrate Reading Objectives 1–6**	25	26 **Assessment Reading Objective**	27
28						

Figure 9

A Case Example for Math

Sun	Mon	Tue	Wed	Thurs	Fri	Sat
Fraction of the week **3/5 60% .6**	1 Continue with math objectives * Integrate Objectives 10 and 13	2	3	4	5 **Assessment Objective 2A, 4a, (metric), 4B, 11A**	6
7 Fraction of the week **1/10 10% .1**	8 Begin math objectives * Integrate Objectives 10 and 13	9	10	11	12	13
Fraction 14 of the week **1/7 14% .14** **Review**	15 Holiday President's Day	16 **Staff Development Day**	17 Continue math objectives Integrate Objectives 10 and 13	18	19	20
Fraction 21 of the week **1/8 13% .13** **Review**	22 **Review for TAAS Writing Test**	23 **TAAS Writing Test**	24 Continue math objectives Integrate Objectives 10 and 13	25	26	27
28			(Continue 2c, 5a, 5b, and 12b into next month)			

Figure 10

Strategies for Success

We recommend the following tips for calendar development:

Emphasize the essentials. When charting calendar objectives, place the emphasis on areas that are compatible with the state reading, writing, and math accountability standards. While everyone supports extracurricular activities, the essentials must come first.

Collaborate. Ask or require teachers to develop their calendars collaboratively and to emphasize core objectives across content areas. This may take a bit longer to coordinate, but the results are well worth the effort.

Disseminate. Distribute and promote the calendar across the campus, so that at any given time, everyone—including students, support staff, and parents—knows what the instructional focus is. For example, post announcements such as:

Grayson Elementary School Weekly Agenda
October 1–5, 2002 Instructional Focus
Math: Objective 10—Estimation
Reading: Objective 6—Point of View: Opinion vs. Fact

Involve everyone. Encourage everyone to support the current instructional focus, from the mathematics teacher to the physical education instructor. This supports the quality concept that "all components of a system work together for the good of the system."

Start early. Allow time in the summer for intensive meetings where teachers can analyze the data, identify priorities, and develop a timeline before the opening of school.

Remember the customer. Plan in-service activities that emphasize high expectations and student performance.

Chapter Reference

Lawrence W. Lezotte, *Creating the Total Quality Effective School*, Effective Schools Products, Inc., 1992.

Chapter 10

DO
Direct the Instructional Focus

"This preoccupation with breadth rather than depth, with quantity rather than quality, probably affects how well U.S. students perform in relation to their counterparts in other countries. It thus determines who are our international 'peers' and raises the question of whether these are the peers that we want to have."
—A Splintered Vision: An Investigation of
U.S. Science and Mathematics Education

Research shows that U.S. public school curriculum and textbooks too often aim for breadth rather than depth by exposing students to many interesting topics but not necessarily resulting in competency or mastery. Depth leads to understanding.

The PDCA Instructional Cycle is about mastery. The next step in the cycle focuses on "Do": the development and delivery of instruction for all subject areas according to the instructional calendar. An in-depth understanding of the accountability standards—the Texas Essential Knowledge Skills (TEKS)—and the TAAS objectives is the goal. To get started, we recommend instructional focus sheets, as illustrated in Figure 11 on page 78, as a valuable tool for defining objectives, target areas, instructional dates, and assessment dates for a given period. The goal is student mastery of the Texas Essential Knowledge Skills. The TAAS objective is to measure proficiency with TEKS.

At Brazosport, teachers whose classes are tested for standards meet over the summer to prepare instructional focus sheets as well as suggested activities to accompany them. The suggestions are a collection of classroom strategies that have worked in the past. When the school year begins, teachers receive a folder each week

Instructional Focus

Subject:	Reading
Objective:	4. The student will perceive relationships and recognize outcomes in a variety of written texts.
Targets:	Relationships and Outcomes
	4a. Understand cause and effect relationships 4b. Predict probable future actions and outcomes
	Integrate: Objectives 1–6
Instructional Dates:	November 4 through December 6
Assessment Date:	December 6
Things to Note:	* Please make sure you have the students justify their answers using the information/clues in the text.
	4a. What will happen when . . . ? _____ ? _____ happened because . . . What causes _____ ?
	4b. How will this story probably end? What probably happened next? After reading this passage, a person will probably . . . What would happen if . . . ? Which of these is the main character most likely to do?

Figure 11

containing the instructional focus sheets as well as the suggested activities for the unit. The teachers are not told how to teach the individual objectives, but rather which objectives must be covered during a particular period. They serve as a blueprint to guide lesson plans.

Because the teachers participated in the calendar development, there are no surprises, and therefore, no resistance. Teachers retain the freedom to use their own ideas, creativity, and personal teaching style to deliver the lesson.

Teaching the Instructional Focus

To ensure that classroom activities stay highly focused and that the classroom climate is conducive to learning, we recommend the following steps:

Highlight the day's focus. Begin the class by posting the current instructional focus and highlighting salient topics. You will catch the students' attention at its peak.

Warm up with a review (8–10 minutes). Review areas previously covered. This serves to warm the students up and reinforce concepts already mastered. It builds on success. Educational theorist Madelyn Hunter describes this activity as the "anticipatory set," a hook that helps focus attention. A good review develops readiness for the next topic and helps students get mentally and physically ready.

Focus on new content (50 minutes). Deliver instruction based on the lesson plan, targeting the area or areas listed on the Instructional Focus Sheet. Instructional focus is the direct teaching of the material on the calendar.

Reinforce the newly learned concepts (20 minutes). Provide guided practice and homework that reinforces the new lesson. Be sure to include a few more problems similar to the warm-up exercises.

Survey the results (10 minutes). Assess student comprehension and provide remedial instruction where necessary.

Notice that the above example calls for a 90-minute class. A number of the schools at Brazosport went to longer classes in language arts and mathematics after they received their TAAS results. The staff members looked at the data and decided their students needed more time in those areas each day. This meant that other subjects, like science and social studies, would meet for 90-minute classes every other day. Why would those teachers agree to this? They realized that their students had to be accomplished in reading, language, and mathematics before they could succeed in their other subjects.

At Brazosport, teachers make every minute count. If you want to insult a teacher there, ask him or her to take a short break from the day's focus. We once called a faculty member to ask if we could take a group picture for a PowerPoint presentation during one of her English classes. There was no response. After a few awkward moments of silence, the teacher politely replied, "No offense, but if it says I teach reading at 10 o'clock in the morning, I will be delivering the instructional focus at that time. You don't need to set up a photo opportunity." This was her time to conduct class business; it was not time for distracting students.

To illustrate how a typical class period works, let us assume it is 10 in the morning and you are the eighth grade math teacher. As your students are seated, you highlight the day's topics, part of a three-week math unit, or you may decide to read the day's instructional focus word for word, just to set the proper "business" tone. You now begin the class by reviewing yesterday's lesson on estimation and calling on all your students, especially those on the periphery. You continually check to make sure your bubble, reteach, and foundation students are with you, asking them questions along the way. You intentionally make a mistake to get a reaction. One student raises her hand: "That is wrong, Miss Smith." You respond, "Oh, it is? Tell me what I should have done."

You are satisfied that everyone understands estimation and is ready to move on to the day's lesson. You know that in addition to your efforts, the concepts have been introduced by physical education, art, and music teachers who reinforced estimation problems with real-life examples the preceding day.

For the next half hour, you delve into the curriculum. You are "on your feet"—actively engaging the class, moving from blackboard to transparency to overhead and checking for understanding. You are modeling strategies used to solve problems. And you are enjoying yourself and making learning fun.

You now guide your pupils through practice and homework that emphasizes the objectives. In the guided practice, you use problems similar to those used in the warm-up. Finally, you assess the results and determine if students understood new concepts and acquired new skills. You provide remedial instruction as needed.

You close the class confident that the school's entire staff will complement your efforts throughout the day. The music teacher, the physical education teacher, and the librarian also have looked at the calendar and have devised their own activities to get these concepts across. The process actually began that morning with the principal's early morning announcements: "Good morning, welcome to Grayson Middle School. The instructional focus this week in reading for sixth grade is … For seventh grade … And for Eighth grade … For Math, the instructional focus for sixth grade is … For seventh grade … And for eight grade …" (Even in Texas, where football is held in the highest esteem, our principals announce the instructional focus before announcing the Friday night football scores on Monday mornings. Now that is saying something!)

Students are exposed to the instructional focus wherever they go. It is posted in the hallways, offices, and in classrooms throughout the campus. The purpose is to underscore the unwritten message: "We mean business. Learning is the most important business on earth. The only reason we exist is for learning and academic performance." This is not meant to diminish developmental activities that teach art, music, physical education, cultural values, and history. Each is essential for a well-rounded education. We are simply saying, "Yes, we believe that your other classes are important, but first and foremost, you must know the standards."

There is no limit to how creative people can be when asked to reinforce the day's instructional focus. There was a bus driver who wouldn't let her passengers off the bus because two students were arguing. She insisted that the students determine what was fact and what was opinion about this argument. "Fact and Opinion" was the focus on the calendar.

Effective Teaching Strategies

The manner in which instruction is delivered to students is key to the PDCA Instructional Cycle. We recommend the following:

Have consistent, high expectations. If students know what is expected, they will deliver. Explain that the role of school is to help students become successful.

Model the way to think about an issue. Both elementary and secondary students need to be taught how to think through a problem. Model your thinking process out loud as you teach. Then, ask students to verbalize their thinking process.

Provide essential vocabulary as you teach math, reading, and writing. If students don't have a strong vocabulary, they can't understand what is being asked of them.

Make learning real. Always relate what you teach to students' lives. Make sure that students also have an appreciation for success that is derived from mastering basic skills.

Use cooperative-learning techniques. All students have something to offer, and students in groups can build on each other's strengths. Students can be great teachers.

Incorporate drill. As skills are taught, they need to be practiced to the point of mastery. Practice makes perfect.

Teach test-taking strategies. Explain that test taking provides a foundation of skills that students will use throughout life: problem solving, process thinking, high-order skills, organization, and handling pressure and stress.

Celebrate mastery of skills and knowledge. Success builds confidence and self-esteem.

More and more teachers we meet are benefiting from the Direct Instruction teaching method. Introduced in 1968 by Siegfried Engelmann, Direct Instruction was first used with inner-city children to help them learn and excel. It is now enjoying renewed popularity as more and more schools are finding it effective for teaching all children. Direct Instruction provides more opportunity for students to participate, more drills, and more content. Teachers who use the method experience rapid and persistent increases in test scores. As an added benefit, students enjoy increased self-esteem and pride in their accomplishments. We recently visited an elementary school in Phoenix that implemented the process and attained a 32-point gain in performance.

Strategies for Success

To ensure that the instructional focus process runs smoothly and effectively, we recommend the following:

Use effective instructional strategies. Follow a plan that helps manage classroom time.

Get everyone involved. Make mastery of the instructional focus areas a schoolwide goal. Disseminate instructional focus sheets that include objectives, target areas, and instructional and assessment dates to all staff members across the entire campus. Use public address announcements to let everyone know that the school's main goal is academic achievement.

Start early. Have the district office order and gather textbooks and other relevant materials so teachers can use them during the summer so they have ample time to prepare thoughtful instructional focus folders.

Solicit feedback from teachers. Take advantage of the keen insight of faculty members; they can make the instructional focus process work best. Allow common planning time in the summer and during the school year to prepare and revise schedules. Use activities that build on the strengths and experiences of other teachers.

Involve the students. Encourage teachers and administrators to ask students in the hallway, "What is the topic of instructional focus this week for your grade?" Keep the instructional focus in everyone's mind to elevate the process from a simple learning experience to a campuswide goal.

Revise activities as needed. Assess student progress on the target objective. If the majority of students are not learning the objective, try a different approach as soon as possible.

Chapter References

William Schmidt, Curtis McKnight, and Senta Raizen, "A Splintered Vision: An Investigation of U.S. Science and Mathematics Education," the U.S. National Research Center for the Third International Mathematics and Science Study, Kluwer Academic Publishers, 1997.

R. Gersten and T. Keating, "Long-Term Benefits from Direct Instruction," *Educational Leadership*, 44(6), 28-29, 1987.

R. Gersten, T. Keating, and W. Becker, "The Continued Impact of the Direct Instruction Model: Longitudinal Studies of Follow Through Students," *Education and Treatment of Children*, 11(4), 318-327, 1988.

Mark Schug, Sara Tarver, and Richard Western, "Direct Instruction and the Teaching of Early Reading," *Wisconsin Policy Research Institute Report*, Vol. 14, No. 2, March 2001.

Chapter 11

CHECK
Assessment

For instruction to be effective, educators must check for understanding. Assessments are the tools we use to tell us how well students are learning and which students need more help.

Frequent assessments produce continuous feedback that enables teachers to make better decisions and to act quickly to improve instruction. They help us teach better. We recommend the strategies listed below to help develop effective assessments for your school or district.

Administer assessments frequently—as often as every two to three weeks—to identify those students who have mastered the objective and those who have not. These can be simple exercises with as few as four questions for each target area. Their purpose is to provide teachers immediate feedback and the opportunity to modify their instruction where needed.

Integrate assessments into the curriculum and instruction. Make sure that your teacher team schedules frequent assessments on the instructional focus calendar. For example, after working on a unit for 14 days, the next day is set aside for assessment, and every student at that grade level is given the same test. Districtwide, the test might be scheduled at different times on different campuses, but all students still take the same assessment. This enables campus and district administrators to compare results on a common standard across classrooms and campuses.

Align assessments with both the content areas of the instructional focus and the accountability standards. Make sure the scheduled assessment is directly related to the unit you have taught as well as the content included on the state assessment. Assessments should have the "look and feel" of accountability tests so students gain experience responding to the test items. When it's time for the real test, students know exactly what is expected of them, and there are no surprises.

Invest in commercial assessments that approximate typical questions on your standards. Good assessments do not rely on a single yardstick. A variety of tests from objective, third parties provide a better measure of true comprehension. They tend to be less predictable, more stimulating, and more challenging. And, when aimed at a slightly higher level of difficulty than the state test items, the tests can do a better job of preparing students for the state-mandated tests. When purchased on a districtwide level, commercial assessments offer the added advantage of letting us use data disaggregation to observe trends throughout the district.

Create teacher teams that meet frequently to review the results of the assessments. Schedule 30- to 60-minute periods for teachers to meet by grade level in elementary and subject level at middle and high school to discuss results. Principals will build this time into the schedule once they realize how critical these reviews are to the quality of instruction. Through collaboration and brainstorming, teachers cannot only identify problems that impede learning but also design creative strategies that reinforce lessons. For example, at Brazosport, language arts teachers decided writing portfolios would help students build skills and trace their own growth and development.

While some may criticize the above approach as "teaching to the test," please note that the vast majority of time, Brazosport teachers are providing direct teaching on the Texas Essential Knowledge Skills. The mini-assessments given every two to three weeks help us learn if students are mastering the state standards. These short tests give students the opportunity to become familiar with the test format and the tools for success. (Obviously, students can't be "taught the test" since standardized tests are secure until the time they are administered.)

To overcome objections of this kind, we recommend that you:

- explain to critics that the accountability standards represent skills that students need to know to become active citizens,

- review actual test items and examples (most critics are impressed with the rigor of these exercises),
- relate real-world applications and real-life examples of student successes from mastering basic skills,
- point to the fact that the "first success" many students experience will have a ripple effect, and
- explain that the school places student success first and feels strongly about the need to prepare students for the state assessment.

Figure 12 is an example of a four-question mathematics assessment for the third grade (Kathy Miller, Kamico Instructional Media, Austin, Texas). It closely matches the format of the state assessment, so students are not tested on something they have not seen.

Mathematics Assessment

1. Each week the Johnson family drinks 12 quarts of milk. How many gallons do they drink?
   A. 4 gal
   B. 3 gal
   C. 2 gal
   D. 1 gal

2. A teacher bought 3 pounds of candy for her students. What is this measure in ounces?
   A. 15 oz.
   B. 30 oz.
   C. 48 oz.
   D. 56 oz.

3. A recipe calls for 24 ounces of chocolate chips. How many cups would that be?
   A. 1 c
   B. 2 c
   C. 3 c
   D. 4 c

4. A fence is 3 inches shorter than 6 feet. How many inches long is the fence?
   A. 36 in.
   B. 48 in.
   C. 57 in.
   D. 69 in.

Figure 12

Teachers walk the class through the questions before administering the test. They then ask them to mark the correct answer and to show their strategy for solving the problem. To get credit for the problem, students can't just mark "a, b, c, or d"; they must show their work. This eliminates the temptation of guessing on multiple-choice answers and makes students better test takers. It also enables the teacher to see the student's thinking process. When teachers review the students' answers, they give a check for each answer that includes the strategy for solving the problem, regardless of whether or not the answer is right.

Although we are not proponents of teaching to the test, we think it's important to give students strategies to help them succeed on district, state, and national assessments. To improve student perform- ance on assessments, share the following test-taking strategies with your classes:

Test-Taking Strategies for Reading

1. Whisper read the title/subtitles. Predict what the passage is about.
2. Carefully study any charts, graphs, or diagrams.
3. Number the paragraphs.
4. Whisper read the questions carefully, circling the key words. Make sure you understand what the question is asking.
5. Beginning with the title, whisper read the passage thoroughly at least two times. Make a mental picture of what is being read.
6. Whisper read the first question and answer choices, getting an idea of what the answer may be. Do not bubble in your answer choice.
7. Return to the passage and underline the clues that support the possible answer.
8. Return to the question and eliminate the wrong answers.
9. Bubble in the correct answer and record the paragraph's number where the answer/clues were located. Remember, you have to prove your answer is correct.
10. Repeat steps 6 through 9 for the remainder of the questions.
11. Check to make sure all questions are answered reasonably.

Test-Taking Strategies for Math

1. Whisper read the problem at least three times. Make a mental picture of what is being read.
2. Circle key words in the question. Make sure you understand what the question is asking.
3. Identify and circle/underline key numbers and labels.

4. Eliminate data that is not needed.
5. Thoroughly study any graphs, charts, or diagrams.
6. Determine the operations/strategies needed to solve the problem.
7. Solve. Show your work. (Draw a picture, label charts and graphs according to the key, fill in place value chart, draw a number line, etc.)
8. Evaluate the solution. Does the solution answer the question? Does the solution make sense?
9. Check your solution with the answer choices. If your answer is not found, repeat steps 1 through 8.
10. Eliminate wrong answers.
11. Bubble in the correct answer.

These strategies ensure that students understand what they are being asked and focus on the heart of the problem. Students learn how to eliminate unnecessary information, highlight clues that can help them solve the problem, and question whether their answer makes sense. While the process may seem tedious at first, in the long run we have found it well worth the effort. Students become better standardized test takers. When they start this process in the first or second grade, by the time they get to fifth grade or higher, taking a test becomes second nature.

After each assessment every two to three weeks, teacher teams meet to review the results. If the students did well as a group, the success is celebrated and the next instructional focus started. If a large number of students did not master the content, the teachers analyze possible causes, make adjustments, and reteach.

Brainstorming and idea sharing produce new ways to get concepts across, and the instructional calendar is adjusted to allow additional time for further emphasis. The next assessment determines if subsequent adjustments are needed and if the new unit can begin.

Summing up the impact of frequent assessments, a fourth grade teacher at Velasco said, "The kids sometimes get tired of the emphasis on testing and results, but they like the feeling of success and achievement that comes with this process."

Measurement Instruments

How do you measure mastery levels and, at the same time, ensure that testing is aligned with instruction and learning? We recommend the use of criterion-referenced tests rather than norm-referenced data to measure student achievement. A combination of criterion-referenced, norm-referenced, and other measures is also useful.

Norm-referenced tests assume standards are distributed by the bell-shaped curve and tell us where a student's performance stands relative to other children. They do not relate overall student proficiency on state or district standards; in fact, the test is considered defective if a majority of students score too well. On the other hand, criterion-referenced tests allow for the possibility that all children can master the standard being tested. Criterion-referenced tests—which are common in law, medicine, and accounting—pinpoint the degree of effectiveness of a district's curriculum and instruction in addressing the standards that are tested.

Brazosport ISD Principal Sam Williams said his school doesn't worry about grades, but instead seeks tests that indicate whether all students are learning. "Providing students with a focus on accountability standards (TEKS) and TAAS objectives provide a foundation for school success. If all students get an "A" because they master all standards, that's OK. In fact, that is our goal."

Larry Lezotte predicts there will be a "shift away from standardized, norm-referenced, paper-pencil tests toward curricular-based, criterion-referenced measures of student mastery." He maintains that data regarding student achievement should relate to instructional objectives and skills identified as essential, not how one student did in relation to another.

Another measure of student achievement is through "alternative"—sometimes called "authentic"—assessments. The goal is to assign projects that encourage independent learning and that demonstrate mastery of content. One example of such an assignment is the writing portfolio or "process-folio" mentioned earlier. The portfolio serves to feature a range of work showing the depth, breadth, and expansion of a student's knowledge over time. It serves as a tool to help the student analyze his or her own development.

Chapter References

Lawrence W. Lezotte and Barbara C. Jacoby, *Sustainable School Reform: The District Context for School Improvement,* Effective Schools Products, Ltd., 1992.

Interview with Clara Sale-Davis and Sam Williams for APQC Baldrige in Education Initiative, May 11, 1999.

Interview with Velasco Elementary fourth grade teachers Hinkle, Cowie, and Conover for APQC Baldrige in Education Initiative, May 11, 1999.

Kathy Miller, Kamico Instructional Media, Austin, Texas, www.kamico.com.

Chapter 12

CHECK
Maintenance

Most of us can remember "cramming" for a test and then quickly forgetting the material when we didn't think we would need it again. Or perhaps we were an expert hula-hooper as a child and do not have a clue of how to keep that thing going round as an adult. Skills that are learned, but not practiced regularly, can be soon forgotten. And yet we teach students in September, and if they forget in April, it's "Gotcha!"

Maintenance helps reinforce skills and knowledge that are taught until they become a permanent part of the student's knowledge base. Maintenance also serves as a reminder that what you have learned has applications in everyday life and you will need it again and again to be successful. Quite simply, "maintenance" in the PDCA Instructional Cycle means helping students retain what they have learned.

Figure 13, page 94, lists the type of maintenance we recommend in the PDCA Instructional Cycle and compares that with traditional methods of maintenance.

Maintenance is particularly powerful when working with economically disadvantaged students. The research shows that at-risk students learn just as well as students in other groups; their IQs are no different. But, when at-risk children go home, little or no reinforcement of school lessons is provided. Once you recognize that this is the source of the problem, you can fix it. ("Don't fix blame; fix the system.")

Maintenance Methods

PDCA Maintenance Measure	Traditional Maintenance
• Maintenance is a district- or schoolwide learning strategy. • Districts or schools provide maintenance materials for the teachers. • Maintenance is ongoing. • Teachers are held accountable for the maintenance activities. • Every student completes all of the maintenance activities.	• Maintenance is up to individual teachers. • Teachers provide their own materials to review instructional topics. • Maintenance is done at the teacher's discretion. • Teachers are not held accountable for maintenance activities. • Maintenance delivery is variable and inconsistent.

Figure 13

To illustrate, let us assume that in September you delivered an effective lesson and that when you checked for understanding, all of the students demonstrated mastery. You wrote down in your grade book, "Everybody mastered." This is where the system usually falls apart. In April, your at-risk kids miss these questions on the state assessment. You ask, "why?" Unfortunately, when they went home, they were not greeted with: "What did you do in school today, honey? Let's talk about it. No TV until you have done your homework. This is a school night … lights out at 9:30." Very few at-risk students go home to that.

The best solution is to assume that everybody is at risk—no matter what the economics—and do the maintenance at school. That's what Brazosport does. Teachers there know they cannot control what happens in students' homes, but they do have control in their classroom. They make maintenance an important part of the instructional process. Maintenance activities are provided all year long in the form of transparencies, booklets, and other materials. Students work individually or as part of a group to complete all of the activities. Maintenance is an important part of the timeline and is part of the daily or weekly routine.

Strategies for Success

- Create maintenance periods that are one week in duration.
- Administer preliminary and post-tests as part of maintenance activities.
- Model what you want the children to learn. You cannot ask students to show you how they solved problems unless you demonstrate the steps, logic, and thought processes to them first.
- Make the maintenance activities fun. Have the students work in cooperative groups; challenge them to create games that test newly acquired knowledge—perhaps based on one of today's popular television quiz shows. Let students create their own problems or invent real-life situations where they must solve a problem. Invite a guest celebrity—perhaps a student from an upper grade, a coach, or principal—to read a passage. Let the students teach the class. The opportunities for fun and creativity are endless.

Chapter 13

CHECK
Monitoring

"Effective principals," Larry Lezotte tells us, "are not just leaders, but instructional leaders, in order that the purpose of the school, that of teaching and learning, can be achieved."

In every way and at every level, the school principal must assume the chief responsibility for monitoring program success. His or her efforts may be complemented by the assistant principal, the district curriculum director, and even the parents and teachers, but it is the principal who must set the tone for the school and spread the word that "Learning is our business." Granted, principals have a myriad of other duties—the day-to-day running of the school, recruitment, paperwork, state compliance, and budgetary concerns. But there is no more important job than providing instructional leadership.

This means principals must spend a good amount of their time in the classroom monitoring learning progress. Monitoring keeps the school's primary business—learning—on track and in focus. It helps foster improved student performance, better discipline, and higher teacher morale.

Through monitoring, the principal seeks to discover what is going well, what is not going well, and what he or she can do to help. The PDCA Instructional Cycle recommends that principals carry out their monitoring responsibilities in the following ways:

- schedule classroom visits on a regular basis;
- schedule one-on-one meetings with students and teachers to review test scores;
- organize celebrations to recognize achievements and gains;

- meet regularly with departments and teams to monitor student progress; and
- use formal and informal surveys to assess processes, school climate, and stakeholder satisfaction.

As a departure from the traditional role of the principal, the effective, quality principal spends a significant amount of time in the classroom and with each student on an individual basis. The purpose is not to check up on teachers or to "snoop," but instead to learn what works, share information with other teachers, and assume the role of guest teacher when appropriate. As the instructional leader of the school, the principal should know what is being taught as well as how it's being taught. In this way, school instruction improves and the principal's role as instructional leader is strengthened. (Chapter 8 discussed the principal's one-on-one role with students through Test Talks.)

An area where Brazosport principals show particularly strong—if not "spirited"—leadership is encouraging students to perform their best for the state assessment. At one event organized by a Brazosport principal, seventh and eighth graders gathered in the gymnasium for an academic pep rally. Wearing team t-shirts, they chanted team cheers to the band's rendition of "Born to be Wild." As the excitement began to build, several of their teachers ran out on the floor carrying a huge run-through banner—the kind normally seen at football games—with the words "Born To Pass TAAS." A few minutes later, students heard a loud engine revving up and, to their amazement, saw their normally conservative principal, Clara Sale-Davis, dressed in black leather, ripping through the sign on a Harley-Davidson. There wasn't a question on anyone's mind that the principal and teachers, perhaps a little crazy, were on their students' team and there to cheer them on.

That principal and others like her do whatever it takes to make students successful. They make it their responsibility to build relationships within the staff and student body so all share a common vision and unite as a team.

When teachers at Velasco Elementary were asked to summarize the leadership characteristics of their principal, Sam Williams, for a Baldrige site visit, they prepared the following list of "Things Sam Does":

- Visits classes regularly
- Builds trust and empowers us—asks teachers how we would solve the problem and supports us with their ideas
- Leads pep rallies
- Listens to teacher and staff suggestions
- Obtains funding and supports fun things, especially to celebrate accomplishments
- Motivates students with pep talks and individual meetings
- Rewards students with game days, lunches, fun times at the mall and local places, painting parties, and beach parties
- Hosts educational field trips, such as "Writing Around Town"
- Maintains a clean and orderly campus

For the same site interview, Brazosport principals Sam Williams and Clara Sale-Davis compiled the following list, providing their personal perspectives of what the principal's key responsibilities are:

- Empower your assistants and staff.
- Model effective instructional techniques.
- Establish and support teams and committees.
- Provide safe, clean, and inviting facilities.
- Deal with discipline decisively and effectively.
- Get people to march with—not behind—you.
- Develop a chemistry with your leadership team.

The two principals also said they do "whatever it takes to get test results," including taking sometimes extraordinary measures to engage even the most troubled student. At times, this has meant personally getting truants out of bed; driving them to school or feeding them; and, when needed, sobering them up. Other times, they have ridden shotgun in police cars the night before testing to enforce curfews and announce TAAS schedules over police bullhorns.

Chapter References

Lawrence W. Lezotte and Barbara C. Jacoby, *Sustainable School Reform: The District Context for School Improvement*, Effective Schools Products, Ltd 1992.

Interview with Clara Sale-Davis and Sam Williams for APQC Baldrige in Education Initiative, May 11, 1999.

Interviews with teachers and coordinators of Brazosport ISD schools, for APQC Baldrige in Education Initiative, May 12, 1999.

Chapter 14

ACT
Tutorials and Enrichment

There was a peculiar irony that summer day in 1991 when the results of the state assessments were first published. It was difficult to accept that so many of the district's at-risk students had failed reading, writing, and mathematics. After all, these students appeared to have plenty of self-esteem, were happy, and actually liked—even loved—many of their teachers. What went wrong?

Looking back, it becomes clear that too many teachers had not expected enough from their students. Patricia Davenport taught English before becoming director of curriculum and instruction. She remembers how often she accepted excuses from her at-risk students because she "felt sorry" for their circumstances:

"Several of my eighth grade students came from really tough neighborhoods. They might come in with, 'Mrs. Davenport, my Dad came in off the road last night and he started drinking and beating up my Mom. We had to go next door, and I didn't get my homework done. Will you give me a break?' And I would say, 'You bet, honey. In fact, let's go get a cold drink and you can talk about it.'"

"Unfortunately, that same student might spend three years in high school as a freshman because she couldn't pass state standards. Or she might drop out of high school and start flipping hamburgers at the local McDonald's.

"There was another teacher students didn't like; in fact, she was despised. When a student came to her with an excuse, she'd say, 'OK, you'll do your assignment at lunch. I'll get you a peanut butter and jelly sandwich. But, I expect to see your homework done today.'

"I was elected Most Popular Teacher three years in a row, while that teacher got no appreciation at all. It occurred to me years later that she was the one who was truly helping our students.

"Before Brazosport teachers were held accountable, many of them were doing all the wrong things for all the right reasons. Yes, we were understanding and let our students know that we cared about their welfare. But, we expected too little. Research shows that students attain the highest level of self-esteem when their teachers set a standard and expect them to meet that standard. Granted, circumstances at home can be less than ideal. But the best gift for these students is to tell them you know they can do better. This may mean having them bring back assignments three or four times, but you don't let them off the hook until they meet the standards. True self-esteem comes when they achieve success."

When Brazosport faculty members and staff became convinced that all students could learn, they did something they had never done before: They refused to allow them to fail.

They raised their expectations and restructured programs accordingly. As a result, the high school with the highest percentage of at-risk students and the lowest writing scores in the district turned itself completely around—eventually surpassing the performance of the district's most affluent high school. Not only did scores improve, but disciplinary referrals declined by about 30 percent and the dropout rate went from 6.7 percent to 0.1 percent in nine years.

Today, if a student wants to drop out, principals, counselors, and teachers alike are unwavering in their response: "No, you're not. We're not going to let you drop out. You will make the greatest mistake of your life if you do." Such students are required to meet with the counselor who searches out the root cause of the imminent dropout and does whatever it takes to dissuade them. If pregnancy is the reason, a number of child-care options are offered. If the student needs a job to help support his family, several options—from preparing for the GED (general education diploma) to attending an alternative school—are suggested.

Team Times—For Mastery and Enrichment

In the past, the assumption was that if students weren't learning, it was their fault. Today we realize there are a variety of reasons why students don't master objectives, many of which are beyond their control. Schools that adhere to quality principles and Effective Schools research take responsibility for student learning and ensure that all students master the essential skills. The PDCA Instructional Cycle maintains that all students can learn through an aggressive program of frequent assessments, maintenance, and tutorials.

The district's first attempt to improve TAAS scores through tutorials didn't work. We made the mistake of scheduling them after school or on Saturdays. When students didn't show up, the staff chalked it up to "Oh, well, we are doing the best we can; we offered the program and they didn't come." Finally, we looked at our data and learned there were some very good reasons students didn't attend, including:

- they didn't have transportation,
- they had young brothers and sisters to baby-sit,
- they had paper routes and other jobs after school, and
- they had parents who had other plans for them and wouldn't let them come.

The schedule had not accommodated our primary customer. Another mistake was in the "packaging." Students thought that tutorials were punishment for not "getting it" in class.

Here's how Brazosport fixed the problem. We believe it will work for your school district as well.

Allot "quality team" periods—a minimum of one each week—for teachers to assess progress and impediments to progress. For middle and high schools, teachers should meet according to subject matter; for elementary school, teachers should meet by grade level. The purpose is to discuss progress in general, review the assessments, and determine which students need "refocusing" through tutorials and which can benefit from enrichment.

Build "team time"—one for tutorials and one for enrichment—into the school day. Let individual schools determine the appropriate time for these. Most schools in Brazosport held them from 2:30 p.m. to 3:30 p.m. daily.

Assign "Team Time" for each student based on frequent assessment results. For example, let us assume we have four sixth-grade math teachers who collectively teach 100 students. Of them, 80 failed the assessment. We take the 80 pupils who failed and divide them into small groups—with no more than 15 in a classroom—to be retaught in team time tutorials. The 20 who passed go to team time for enrichment. For the next assessment, perhaps only 40 students require tutorial team time and the remaining 60 can go to enrichment team time. The number of students in each group is constantly changing.

"Repackage" tutorials as a positive way to achieve mastery. Talk to your students in an adult and encouraging way about the opportunity to participate in team time tutorials. There is no need to mention that they happen to be the youngest person in the class or that there are family issues. Simply say, "Based on your test results, certain standards have not yet been learned." Put the blame on the teaching. "For whatever reason there is a gap here and we are going to fix it. We are going to provide team time so you can be successful." That moves away from "You are dumb" to "We didn't teach you."

Don't sacrifice excellence for equity. Don't make the mistake of focusing only on tutorials and "hanging the other kids out to dry." Enrichment needs to be a priority, too. Without it, parents would have every right to object, "I don't want my child spinning his wheels for 30 minutes just to get the other kids to grade level."

Use new materials for enrichment. Don't use the same materials for enrichment classes that you use during your regular classes. Budget funds for each campus to purchase different and more challenging materials. Mastery students respond to higher-order thinking skills, just as gifted students do. Use gifted and talented teachers as a resource for recommending materials and strategies for enrichment.

Encourage mastery students to go beyond. Students who consistently go to enrichment need new challenges. Give them an opportunity to attend an additional elective or advanced placement course. Or allow mastery students to attend a local college during the day to earn college credit. At Brazosport, many students are now earning their diploma from the local high school and working toward their associate's degree from the local community college at the same time.

Rotate staff members between enrichment and tutorials. Most school systems think only math, English, or reading teachers can teach those courses. Because small class sizes are critical, at Brazosport everyone "teaches"—coaches, physical education instructors, librarians, the principal, the assistant teacher, parents, and even older students. Students also enjoy the change when we break barriers from traditional teaching assignments. Shift everyone around; let gifted education teachers work with nonmastery students, music teachers cover math reviews, and special education teachers provide enrichment. Who teaches each group is up to your school. But remember that the system seems to work best when traditional roles are broken down. The idea is for the student in the math tutorial to go home and say, "The music teacher showed us how to work our math problems and also how you need math to write music. It was cool."

Involve parents whenever possible. Parents are ideal choices for additional tutors or for leading enrichment programs. Invite them to serve as teachers and teacher assistants. For enrichment classes, ask parents to design curriculum that stretches students' minds—like solving a problem or puzzle, designing a technology, or learning how to prepare for an unusual career path.

The Rewards of Continuous Improvement

While some nonmastery students will spend most of the year in tutorials, others tend to spend more and more time in enrichment. Initially, Brazosport had about 80 percent of its students in tutorials. Nine years later, 80 percent were in enrichment. That's one of the rewards of continuous improvement.

Even for those students who are in tutorials year-round, there is no feeling of resentment or penalty. There is no stigma. Before the system was put into place, coming in after school could be very traumatic. Today, tutorials are scheduled during regular hours, and students understand why they are there. They have been told, "The benchmarks are showing us there is something we have not yet taught you. We are going to teach you that this year." They are usually eager to have a chance to catch up.

Do parents fault the teacher when their child spends so much time in tutorials? They can be very understanding when it is explained that tutorials serve to reinforce and extend what is learned in class. Make it clear that tutorials are for reinforcement and that we want to be sure your child doesn't forget. Also explain that different activities and teachers are used. The music teacher may do the team time for the math teacher. This "change of scenery" is stimulating, fun, and rewarding.

Extended Day—A Superior Alternative to Summer Programs

In addition to team time for tutorials during the day, Brazosport uses an "extended day" intervention program. Before getting to this point, students were threatened with, "If you don't pass standards, you are going to summer school. And, if you don't come to summer school, you are not going to the next grade. You may have A's and B's in your classes, but you must come to summer school for standards."

Neither the students nor the teachers looked forward to it. Students wanted to enjoy the summer like everyone else. The teachers were there for the extra income summer sessions provide. It was punishment for all. So, no one was really surprised when we looked at the data from the initial summer school effort and found no measurable improvement. On those few occasions when a student who attended summer classes actually passed standards, the credit went to the classroom teacher, not to what took place over the summer.

Teachers at one middle school proposed an idea to change this. They asked the superintendent to let them teach standards after school for the three-week period before the TAAS test was administered. "You told us to think outside the box, and we have," they said. "For the same amount you'd spend for summer school, we'll develop and teach an after-school intervention program for the three weeks before the test, Monday through Thursday. If it works like we think it will, we won't need summer school anymore."

Gerald thought the idea had merit. For some time, he had been harping on everyone to think outside the box and to take a risk. The teachers delivered and got the go-ahead.

The program worked liked this: Each teacher had 10 students grouped by standard, nonmastery level. They met from 3:30 p.m. to 5:30 p.m. Monday through Thursday for three weeks before the test. As an incentive, snacks and transportation home on the bus were provided. The first year, vegetables and fruit were served; the following year it was pepperoni pizza and sodas every day for 14 days. (The sodas were donated, and pizza was purchased at cost.) Not only did nonmastery students come for pizza and sodas, but mastery students came for them as well and were put to work as tutors.

Each day after school, students and teachers took their pizza break first in the cafeteria. Teachers then took their 10 students to their respective classrooms to review objectives that were not yet mastered. Just as in the regular tutorials, teachers were rotated, so students were assigned to someone other than their regular classroom teacher.

The result? Some 92 percent of kids considered to be "on the bubble" passed the state assessment that year and the school became "recognized." Other schools in the district have followed suit over the years, and today there is no longer summer school to help students master the TEKS anywhere in the district. Today, if you ask the participants why they enroll in extended day, they don't hesitate, "Man, for the pizza." For the at-risk students, it is something special. They may come for the pizza, but they leave with new skills. Not a bad exchange.

For your district, you may want to try extended day before or after school or on Saturdays. If you choose mornings, serving a good breakfast may be in order. If you schedule intervention in the afternoon, pizza is always a winner. Find the funds in the budget. Let the staff determine what else will attract your customer—the student—to the program. You will find, as we did, that the most creative ideas come from teachers.

Epilogue

We have been telling our story for about five years now—at first on an informal basis and now as full-time trainers and consultants.

On a number of occasions, seminar participants have urged us to put the information together in book form. "I'm not going to remember everything, and I'd like to take this back to share with my colleagues," many have said. They suggested that we make it simple and write it down just the way we tell it.

So, with their encouragement and the persistence of Jack Grayson, chairman of APQC, that is exactly what we have tried to do. Ours is a story of change. It begins with the external factors that made it clear that we were not doing a good job with at-risk students and then recounts the steps we took to make the educational process work for every student in our district.

These pages were not intended to be a substitute for either a theory or methods text, but to take you down familiar hallways with new eyes and a practical, common-sense approach for managing schools. We are reasonably certain that you can identify with our experiences, from the challenges inherent in working with at-risk students to the frustration of dealing with irate parents. We hope to provide you with some new ideas and tools that can help your school or district improve. Finally, it is our sincere wish that you find the process enjoyable, because what we do is fun and so very rewarding.

Of course, we focused on the Brazosport Independent School District and the tools that were used to implement change there. Two obvious questions remain: What happened to Brazosport after we left? And how is the PDCA model working at other schools?

Continuous Improvement at Brazosport

The great news about TQM is, once set in motion, improvement continues. As in all things, leadership is critical to keep the effort focused and standards high. The current superintendent of Brazosport Independent School District and his staff are to be commended for their continued commitment to quality and excellence.

Today, the following belief statements are posted on Brazosport's Web site:

- We can teach all students.
- All children can learn, given the appropriate time and resources.
- Leadership must focus all members of the organization on its vision.
- Continuous, measurable improvement is critical to realizing the vision.
- We can provide resources in a cost-effective manner.

Brazosport ISD continues to earn the Texas Education Agency's (TEA's) distinction as an exemplary school district, bestowed only when 90 percent or more of the students in a district, including all subgroups, pass the TAAS exams in reading, writing, and mathematics. Brazosport ISD is the largest district in the state to earn this recognition.

Figures 14, 15, and 16 (pages 111 and 112) show the trend lines of Brazosport students in reading, math, and writing for the period from 1992 through 2001. The numbers speak for themselves; the district continues to close the gap in student achievement.

The district's new vision is to be "exemplary and beyond" in response to TEA's expanded curriculum requirements, which now include science and social studies in addition to English language arts and mathematics, as part of the Texas Essential Knowledge and Skills (TEKS). The district has also put renewed emphasis on "writing, writing, writing."

Current goals for the district include:

- ensuring that all students master TEKS on future TAAS tests,
- increasing enrollment in advanced placement courses,
- increasing concurrent enrollment in credit courses at the local community college (More than 400 students currently participate in the district-funded program.),
- increasing ACT/SAT scores,
- increasing the number of high school students enrolled in the state-recommended course of study,

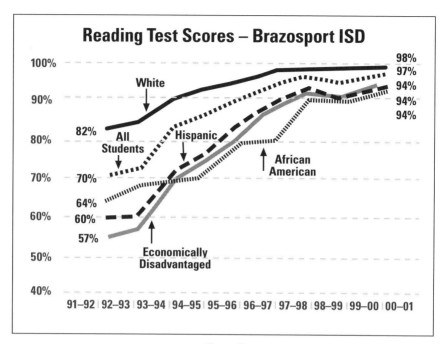

Figure 14

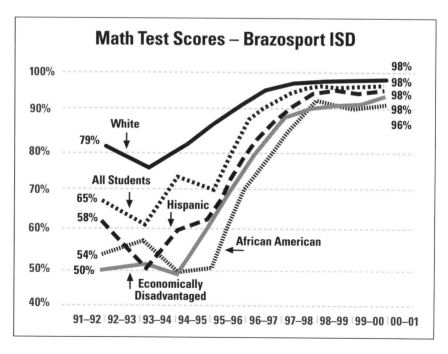

Figure 15

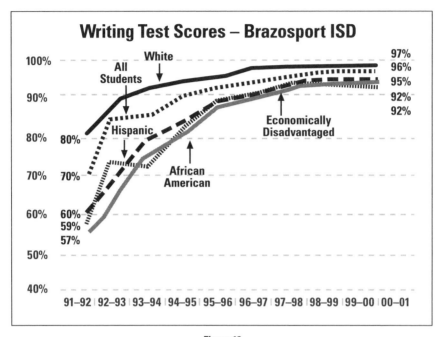

Figure 16

- increasing the number of graduates going to college,
- improving all students' technology skills, and
- achieving a zero percent dropout rate (which currently stands at less than 1 percent.)

The district is flooded with calls from so many educators wishing to learn from Brazosport's example that the board of education has found it necessary to limit such visits to a few days a year so teachers and students don't get distracted.

Replicating the System and Strategies at Other Schools
The PDCA Instructional Cycle is intended to be flexible and to improve with new ideas and experiences. We are seeing trends that tell us when educators adapt the system to meet their particular needs, success is usually not far off. The key is to have a vision and a belief that all children can learn, to set high expectations, and to construct an aligned strategic planning process. Once in place,

ongoing teacher collaboration is critical and most effective when data and quality tools are part of the process.

But we can only say so much. Following is a sampling of what several educators have discovered with these methods. We think their own words are the most convincing case for support.

Fontana Unified School District—Fontana, California

"Fontana Unified School District began using the PDCA Instructional Cycle in August 2000. Fontana and APQC selected several pilot schools (Focus on Achievement schools) to launch the project. Patricia Davenport and Gerald Anderson conducted intensive training in the PDCA Cycle and Effective Schools. Through periodic process check activities involving APQC staff members, schools continue to enhance the aligned goals of closing the gap in student performance and maximizing the efforts of teachers and staff. Fontana has dedicated four lead teachers to develop instruction manuals for K–12 that include instructional focus activities, assessments, and tutorial/reteach activities based on the California standards and state assessment criteria." (Figure 17a and Figure 17b, page 114)

— Dr. Karen Harshman, Superintendent, Fontana Unified School District

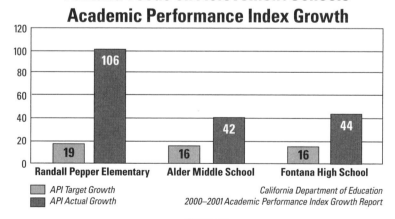

Fontana Focus on Acievement Schools'
Academic Performance Index Growth

API Target Growth
API Actual Growth

California Department of Education
2000–2001 Academic Performance Index Growth Report

Figure 17a

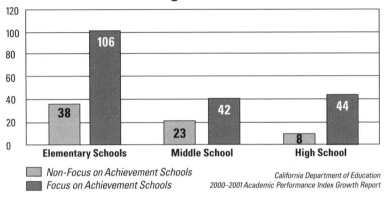

**Fontana Unified School District
Average API Growth**

Figure 17b

Charlotte-Mecklenburg Schools—Charlotte, North Carolina

"APQC began working with Charlotte-Mecklenburg Schools (CMS) in 2000. Gerald Anderson and Patricia Davenport completed training with their A+ school districts, and other APQC staff delivered training in quality tools and problem solving. Test results are showing an improvement in student achievement. Thomasboro came up over 40 points in fifth grade reading. There are some grade levels at a few schools that made minimal growth, but the reasons can be identified. Districtwide reading scores in 5th grade are up to 82 percent above grade level."

> — Dr. Francis Haithcock, associate superintendent
> for educational services,
> Charlotte-Mecklenburg Schools

Aldine Independent School District—Aldine, Texas

"Aldine was one of the first school systems to benchmark the best-practice instructional cycle from Brazosport. Aldine is also now working with APQC to use a Baldrige-based assessment to identify performance gaps and improve its central office processes. The data from Aldine charts its students' growth on the Texas Assessment of

Academic Skills (Figure 18). Aldine is closing the gap across all student groups."

— Nadine Kujawa, superintendent,
Aldine Independent School District

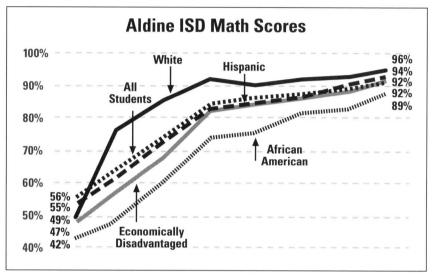

Figure 18

Center Unified School District—Antelope, California

"In 1997 the Center Unified School District adopted a new standards-based language arts curriculum in grades K–6 and set a goal of having 80 percent of all students at or above grade level in reading. A cadre of five reading coaches worked with the K–6 teachers to improve instructional delivery. To track and document progress toward this ambitious goal, forms were developed to record the results of frequent assessments in a variety of areas, including fluency, comprehension, vocabulary, skills, and spelling. A plan to review the assessment results at the site and district level monthly was also put in place.

"Faculty agreed to pace the curriculum similarly at each site with all teachers using the same materials. The implementation was our 'do' stage. Collecting the assessment data monthly was our 'check.' Students falling below the criterion score on any assessment were targeted during a daily workshop (small group or 1:1 instructional session). Class demos, lesson-planning help, taking teachers to watch colleagues, and peer support made up our 'act.' Scores began to rise immediately. By 2001, after an expansion of the PDCA cycle to secondary English and math, every grade level from 2 to 11, scored significantly higher than both the state and the county in the areas of reading, math, language, and spelling (Figure 19).

"We feel our implementation of the PDCA cycle, along with a uniform, standards-based curriculum with a strong monitoring and intervention component, was responsible for the districtwide success for all our students."

— Dr. Lois Ortmann, literacy coordinator, and
Jan Adams, assistant superintendent,
Center Unified School District

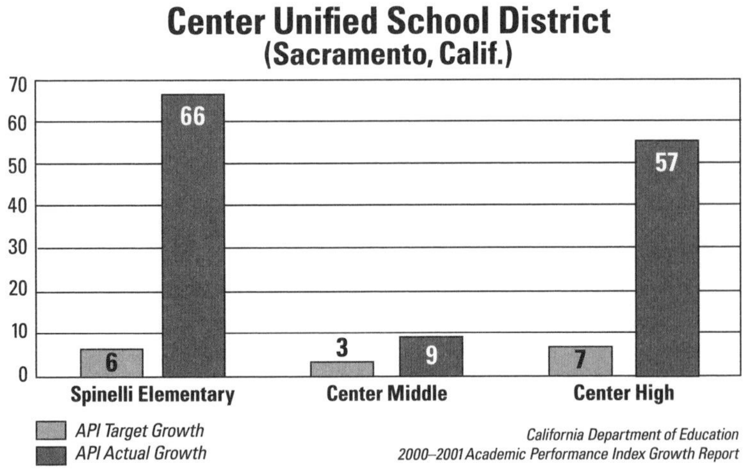
Center Unified School District
(Sacramento, Calif.)
70
60
50
40
30
20
10
0
6
66
3
9
7
57
Spinelli Elementary
Center Middle
Center High
API Target Growth
API Actual Growth
California Department of Education
2000–2001 Academic Performance Index Growth Report

Figure 19

Rio Rancho Public Schools—Rio Rancho, New Mexico

"The Rio Rancho Public Schools have improved in every grade level and content area on norm-referenced state-mandated test results. There are still some gaps, but school officials are very pleased with the first year of implementation. Four of six elementary campuses that embraced the instructional process did quite well. All of the middle schools did well (with some identifiable gaps), as did the high school. One elementary school, Puesta del Sol, the district's most diverse and disadvantaged school, transformed itself from the district's lowest achieving school to its highest, attaining a rating of "exemplary" for the 2001–2002 school year (Figure 20). I have used the instructional process as a high school principal and have implemented it from the district perspective as well. I recommend the approach for districts that use either a criterion- or norm-referenced test as their state's primary assessment and accountability instrument."

— Dr. Manuel Rodriguez, associate superintendent,
Rio Rancho Public Schools

Puesta del Sol Elementary
Fourth Grade CTBS Scores

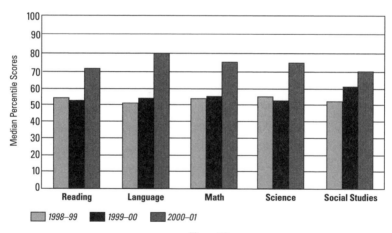

Figure 20

Willis Independent School District—Willis, Texas

"APQC began working with Willis Independent School District in 1999 to help the district improve its rating from "recognized" to "exemplary." The Willis ISD board and I endorsed the implementation of the PDCA Instructional Cycle and training for all administrators and lead staff in Quality Tools and Instructional Leadership.

Gerald Anderson, Patricia Davenport, and Olivea Suazo led monthly in-service sessions and PDCA activities. Willis High School moved from 'acceptable' to 'exemplary' in one year and student achievement throughout the district continues to improve."

— Kay Karr, superintendent,
Willis Independent School District

Wood Elementary—Tempe, Arizona

"Two years ago the Wood Elementary staff endorsed the PDCA model. The school has a 'minority majority' student population with the largest ethnic groups composed of Native Americans and Hispanics—some of whom do not speak English in their homes. One of the larger of 24 schools in the urban district of Tempe, Wood Elementary had, until recently, consistently ranked near the bottom on all achievement measures.

"Using Math Team Times and Language Labs at grades 1–5, Wood within one year achieved significantly higher levels on all testing measures required by the state and district. (These measures include Stanford 9, Northwest level tests, Arizona Instructional Measurement of Standards, and District Assessment Program components.) Both the staff ('PDCA makes sense ... it's good for students') and students ('I'm learning things in math that even my parents don't know!') were elated with the improvement in test results (Figure 21).

"With our School Improvement Process, we revisit our model each spring after school dismisses for the year and again in August before we begin the school year. We share and analyze test data—looking for our strengths and needs. Curriculum calendars are developed during the summer. These calendars reflect Arizona standards, district curriculum, and the various test data. The calendars remain a working plan for instruction during the school year. The calendars focus learning activities, assure all standards are covered, and encourage teamwork at grade levels. Special area resource teachers work with grade levels to implement the same standards for identified students. Librarian, PE, and other staff members are expected to teach standards in their respective settings. Teaching assistants and student teachers are used to maintain small groups for tutorial, maintenance, and enrichment components. We are very proud of our improved student achievement."

— Nancy S. Haugen, principal,
Wood Elementary

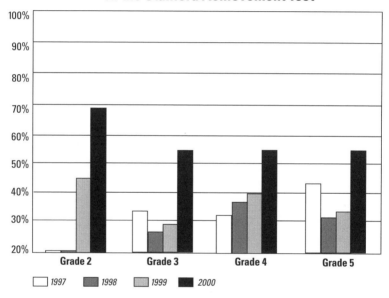

Wood Elementary School
Mean Percentile Ranks for Total Math
on the Stanford Achievement Test

Figure 21

A Few, Final Thoughts

Mike Schmoker, an author and school improvement consultant, was asked to provide his perspective on the PDCA Instructional Cycle and if he thought it was transferable. His comments, presented in their entirety, follow.

Patricia Davenport and Gerald Anderson accom-
plished something truly exceptional in Brazosport schools.
They helped to lead and create one of the best, most results-

oriented improvement systems I know of. And, like the best schools and districts, their effort is marked by simplicity. As a consultant and as a student of what it takes to improve schools, I deeply admire such simplicity—carried out with heart and energy.

They and their colleagues knew that the soul of school improvement is collective teacher expertise aimed at stubborn, low-performing areas of achievement—identified using readily available assessment data. So they made time for teachers to meet, to refine instruction in targeted areas, and work toward measurable achievement goals. The story of Brazosport is a dramatic one. It starts with the discovery of one teacher, whose exceptional success became the catalyst for further discoveries as first a few and then more and more teachers and administrators found and refined simple structures and strategies that could ensure that virtually every kid learned essential standards.

The best part of the story is that any school could adapt or replicate the essential features of their program—built as they are around the PDCA (Plan, Do, Check, Act) cycle. In education, that means: Put teams of educators together, let them invent better ways to teach difficult skills and standards, and refine the lessons and strategies through trial and error—through ongoing assessment. As Davenport likes to stress, it's amazing we haven't been doing such simple, obvious things for decades.

Brazosport's success is a tribute to collective teacher expertise, organized and led by exceptional leaders like Gerald Anderson and Patricia Davenport. Their success is among the defining moments in the history of public education.

It is always gratifying—and humbling—when a respected colleague, such as Dr. Schmoker, offers such a kind appraisal of our work. However, the greatest rewards come when we hear from districts with which we have visited and learn of their successes. It is simply thrilling to return to a district and marvel at the innovative ways they have put the PDCA cycle to work to fit their own circumstances.

Of course, hailing from Texas makes some of these visits all the sweeter. We will never forget the warm welcome we received not long ago upon returning to Center Unified School District in Antelope, California just outside of Sacramento. A year earlier, Pat had met for just a half day with the district's principals. On this visit, all the teachers, principals, and the superintendent greeted us in the auditorium with Lyle Lovett's rendition of a "Long Tall Texan" resonating in the background. There was a terrific rally from the teachers, a huge school banner held high displaying the number of points' increase in test scores, and a huge "Thank you, Pat Davenport." We didn't do the work. All we did was provide a four-hour overview with principals. But the principals took the process back to school and said, "We can do this."

Other participants go back and very quietly put the process into place. We may not hear from them for two or three years, but when we do, it may be a call saying, "We went back, we disaggregated our data, and we developed a time line. Our scores are way up."

Not all of your efforts will reap rewards immediately. What we were able to achieve in year five far surpassed our often rocky beginnings. Adapting the process takes time, perseverance, and determination. But, no matter how lengthy or how involved the investment becomes, there is no greater dividend than seeing a child's face when a new concept has been discovered and understood. At that moment, a lifetime of possibility opens. That's really what this is all about.

Our message to all remains simple and our enthusiasm unabashed. *We did it. It works. You can do it, too.*

Reference

"Brazosport Independent School District, Clute, Texas, TQM + Effective Schools + 8-Step Process = No More Gap!" *High Student Achievement: How Six School Districts Changed Into High-Performance Systems,* Educational Research Service, 2001, Arlington, Virginia.

About the Authors

Patricia Davenport

Patricia Davenport works with the Education Initiative of the American Productivity & Quality Center in addition to serving as a private educational consultant. Her focus is to support individual schools and districts in their efforts to achieve systemic change through the integration of an instructional process, quality, and effective schools research.

Prior to becoming an educational consultant, Davenport was a key leader of a dramatic change initiative to close the gap in student achievement within Brazosport Independent School District in Freeport, Texas. She served at Brazosport for 30 years—13 years as a classroom teacher, seven years as a school counselor, and 10 years as an administrator. Davenport served as director of curriculum and instruction during the last five years of her tenure and directed the implementation of an instructional process that resulted in achievement parity on the state assessment across all student groups.

Davenport received a bachelor of science degree in education from Southwest Texas State University and earned a master's degree in education from the University of Houston. In addition, she holds a mid-management certification and is a licensed professional counselor. A nationally known keynote and featured presenter who leads training in individual schools and districts across the nation, Davenport has two children, John and Kate, and resides in Houston, Texas.

Gerald E. Anderson

Former co-director of the American Productivity & Quality Center's Education Initiative, Gerald E. Anderson, Ed.D., recently established the Equity, Excellence and Quality Center, the mission of which is to close the achievement gap among all students in the United States.

Anderson made his mark as superintendent of Brazosport Independent School District, a 14,000-student district in an industrialized region on the Texas Gulf Coast, beginning in 1991 after top administrative positions at Taft and Brenham school districts in Texas. During Anderson's tenure, which ended with his retirement in July 2000, the district made remarkable strides in student achievement.

Believing that W. Edwards Deming's teachings could be applied successfully in public schools, Anderson began to train central office staff members and principals in quality practices. As a result of hard work and continual focus on a core belief that all children could learn, given the time and resources, Brazosport became the first school district to win the Texas Award For Performance Excellence.

More than 90 percent of all student groups in each of the district's 18 schools—White, Hispanic, African American, rich, and poor—passed the Texas Assessment of Academic Skills (TAAS). Because of its TAAS accomplishments, low dropout rate, and high attendance rate, Brazosport was recognized as "exemplary" by the Texas Education Agency.

Anderson came up through the ranks of Texas community colleges, receiving his associate of arts degree from Weatherford Junior College in Weatherford, Texas. After receiving a bachelor's degree in mathematics from Texas Tech University and a master's degree in education administration from Tarleton State University, he obtained his doctorate in education administration at Texas A&M University. Anderson has two children, Paige and Brock.

About APQC's Education Initiative

A recognized leader in benchmarking, knowledge management, measurement, process improvement, and quality, the American Productivity & Quality Center helps organizations adapt to rapidly changing environments, build new and better ways to work, and succeed in a competitive marketplace. For the past 25 years, APQC has been identifying best practices, discovering effective methods of improvement, broadly disseminating findings, and connecting individuals with one another and with the knowledge, training, and tools they need to succeed.

In 1997 APQC launched its Education Initiative with a mission to ensure equity and excellence for all students regardless of race, gender, or socioeconomic background. Since then, APQC has worked with hundreds of districts and education organizations across the nation to improve student and system performance. APQC is a member-based nonprofit serving more than 500 organizations around the world in all sectors of business, education, and government. Learn more about APQC's Education Initiative by visiting www.apqc.org/education or calling 800-776-9676 or 713-681-4020.